Moving The Hand Of God

**Putting Memorial Prayer
to Work for You**

Moving The Hand Of God

**Putting Memorial Prayer
to Work for You**

by
John Avanzini

HARRISON HOUSE
Tulsa, Oklahoma

Unless otherwise indicated, all Scripture quotations are taken from the *King James Version* of the Bible.

Moving the Hand of God —
Putting Memorial Prayer to Work for You

ISBN 0-89274-861-3

Cover design by Bob Haddad

Published by Harrison House, Inc.
P. O. Box 35035
Tulsa, Oklahoma 74153

*This book is lovingly dedicated
to my wife, Patricia,
who is my partner in life
and in the revelation of this message.*

Contents

Introduction

Being a child of the Most High God is the greatest privilege a human being can receive. However, if that child cannot get his prayers answered, it is painful to say the least. As close as the new birth has made him to his God, unanswered prayer can drive a wedge between the Father and His disappointed child.

Unanswered Prayer Everywhere

You would think that unanswered prayer would be almost unheard of in the Body of Christ. But everywhere I go I meet bona fide children of God who cannot seem to get God to respond to their requests.

To prove to myself that my observation is true, I test congregations from time to time. I ask them if there are any in attendance who have urgent prayer needs that are not being met. Every time I do, the response is the same. Without hesitation, the greater part of the crowd will raise their hands.

Please do not misunderstand. I'm not saying that God never answers prayer. Innumerable times He most definitely does answer the prayers of His children. Every Christian I know has glowing testimonies of special requests God has answered.

As for my own prayer requests, I thank God for the many petitions He has graciously answered for me. I also thank Him for every request He has granted others. However, with all that said, it is still painfully evident that many urgent requests are never fulfilled.

For many years all I could do when this dilemma faced me was to give some canned answer I had learned in Bible college. Not only was I constantly confronted by those who were not getting their prayers answered, but many of my own prayers were also unanswered.

Like others, I would fervently and sincerely pray, only to see my worst fears come to pass. Once my car was repossessed. Another time the finance company took back the home we lived in. Even the precious lives of saints I prayed for would slip beyond the veil of death. It seemed to me that when I prayed, it became a tossup as to whether or not God's hand would move in the matter. More times than I like to remember, the eleventh hour came and went without even the slightest evidence of the divine intervention I had been seeking. How often I wished there were a way I could consistently move the hand of God on my behalf.

Life-Changing Events Are Just Ahead

Do not think this is a book of defeat. It is anything but that. This is a book of victory, for there is most definitely a way for God's children to move His hand consistently. In fact, our great God actually invites us to direct the work of His hands. This statement is not just the good idea of a man, but it is the literal Word of God.

> **. . . concerning the work of my hands**
> *command ye me.*
> **Isaiah 45:11**

You are about to learn a well-proven Bible method of getting God's attention. Not only can you focus His attention to the point of your greatest need, but you will also learn how to move His hand to meet that need. Instead of continually facing the disappointment of unanswered prayer, you will begin to live in the satisfaction of having your God move the mountains you face.

The next hours we spend together in the Word of God will reveal a precious piece of information. You will look back on the time spent reading this book and receiving its truth as one of the most profitable experiences of your life.

1

Unanswered Prayer — A Church-Wide Scandal

. . . concerning the work of my hands command ye me.

Isaiah 45:11

From the beginning of this book I want it made perfectly clear that I believe God answers prayer. I also want to make it clear that the method of prayer I am about to teach you is by no means the only one taught in God's Word. The Bible speaks of several different types of prayer.

Effective prayer does not have to be *complicated prayer.* Sometimes just a simple request spoken under one's breath brings quick results. Sometimes a group prayer moves God. Sometimes only after some special person prays, such as the pastor or an evangelist, God answers. Other times the answer comes only after fasting has been added to the prayer.

Please understand, I am not seeking to change the prayer methods of those who consistently get answers to prayer. I am trying to help those whose prayers are seldom answered. I want to help them into a totally biblical method of prayer — a method that always works for those who properly use it.

We Will Search The Scriptures

This book will take you step by step through the Scripture. It will show you that there have always been people who knew how to direct the hand of God quickly to their needs and wants. The method of prayer I refer to is so different from traditional prayer that it will take the greater part of this book to open your spirit and effectively reveal it.

The Revelation Came In A Special Way

This special revelation was given to me by God as I sought a reason for unanswered prayer in the life of a former church member. This dear man was faced with a desperate situation, but no matter how hard he tried, his prayers were bringing forth absolutely no results.

It all took place during a time when I was satisfied with the stale answers of Bible commentators. I can still remember those uneventful days. Whenever difficult questions arose, I would carefully read through my commentaries and choose the answer I liked most. Then I would piously use that answer as if it were my own. When it came to explaining why prayers were not answered, I found the words of a commentator I especially liked. He explained why God didn't answer prayer in this way. He said, "God always answers every prayer. The problem most Christians face is that they don't realize God has three possible answers to every prayer request. They are 'yes,' 'no,' and 'later.'"

I remember how much I liked that answer. In fact, I thought it was the perfect answer! It was smart sounding, and it fit every possible prayer situation. If God immediately granted a request, that answer was correct, for God had evidently said, "*Yes.*" If for some reason an extra long time passed before the prayer was fulfilled, no doubt God had said, "*Later.*" After a much longer wait, if it became obvious that the prayer was never going to be answered, I could tell people God had said, "*No.*" For longer than I like to admit, that was my standard response to those who had trouble getting their prayers answered.

My Canned Answer Was Ready

One day that special church member I mentioned asked me why God was not answering an important prayer request he was faithfully bringing before Him. He assured me that everything was right in his heart and life. He related that his request was totally in line with the Word of God. He knew exactly what needed to be done. However, each day it seemed as if his faithful prayer was falling on deaf ears. He made it clear to me that his unanswered prayer was not only bringing suffering to the Kingdom of God, but severely damaging his own family.

Even before he finished speaking, I had already decided what my reply would be. I felt he would be excited when he heard the great wisdom in my answer. I told him he would have to be ready for one of three answers from God: "yes," "later," or "no." After giving him that wisdom, I felt I would be free of further responsibility with his problem. It would automatically be back on his shoulders instead of on mine.

When A Canned Answer Won't Do

Before I could walk away, he abruptly stopped me by sternly saying, "Brother John, please don't give me that standard explanation of yours. I am in no mood for *canned answers.* I need to know two very important things. First, *how do I get God's attention* before this thing destroys me and my family? Secondly, *how do I direct the hand of God* to a solution to my problem?"

His words, "*How do I direct the hand of God?*" exploded in my mind. I knew I had heard or read those same words somewhere before. I also realized that he already knew exactly what needed to be done. His solution was right in line with God's Word, but *absolutely nothing was happening when he prayed.* Realizing the depth of his concern and the pitiful weakness of my answer, I promised him I would immediately go to the Word of God and find the biblical solution for his problem.

The Search For God's Answer

That night I began to diligently search the Word of God. After some effort, I found the verse of Scripture I was looking for. I had marked it several years before and had made a note by it that simply said, "How wonderful this would be if it could be done." This is what the verse said:

> **Thus saith the Lord, the Holy One of Israel, and his Maker, Ask me of things to come concerning my sons, and** *concerning the work of my hands command ye me.*
>
> **Isaiah 45:11**

There it was! "Concerning the work of my hands command ye me." Even though I had read it before, it still sounded strange to me. It seemed wrong even to suggest that God would invite us to direct the work of His mighty hands.

As I was prone to do in those days, I went immediately to my favorite commentaries for an answer. However, after carefully reading each comment, I found that instead of giving me an explanation, they simply tried to explain the verse away.

It Checked Out In The Original Language

Upon checking the original language of the verse, I came to the conclusion that the *King James Version* correctly interpreted the original text. What the King

James translators had written was exactly what the prophet Isaiah had said. The great God, Jehovah, was inviting His children into a most personal relationship with Him. He was literally asking them to begin ruling and reigning with Him.

God Wants Partners

With that information in hand, I started an expanded study into the strange request of the verse. I began to investigate exactly why we, the created, were being asked to direct the hand of our great God.

Within just a short period of study time, I began to realize that most church leaders were making a big mistake in their directions to the body of Christ. The error was in the form of two wrong instructions they were giving. Some church leaders were teaching people that they were to become the *slaves of God.* Others were teaching them the exact opposite. They were saying *God was to become our slave.* Upon closer examination of God's Word, I found that He wasn't waiting for us to give Him a job, nor was He trying to give us a job. I found that God was looking for people who would go to *work with Him.* He was actually calling His born-again ones into *partnership with Him. What He wanted was for us to rule and reign with Him.*

Remember, we are called to be *joint heirs with Christ.*

The Spirit itself beareth witness with our spirit, that we are the children of God:

And if children, then heirs; heirs of God, and *joint-heirs with Christ.* . . .
Romans 8:16,17

Suddenly the words, "concerning the work of my hands command ye me," didn't seem quite so strange. In fact, Isaiah's words seemed quite reasonable if we are co-laborers, or even better, *co-rulers with Him.* In a relationship of that kind it would be a common occurrence for us to direct His hand.

Keep Looking Down

When that thought was firmly fixed in my thinking, I realized that the old saying, "Keep looking up," was not a scriptural one. I would have to be out of place to keep looking up. Remember, God has invited all of His children to be seated with Him in heavenly places at His right hand with Jesus. If I positioned myself to keep looking up, I would have to be beneath my appointed place. I would have to be at ground level, in the middle of the battle with only a limited view of what was happening. From that substandard position, I could not hope to grasp the problem well enough to direct the hand of God.

However, if I were where I belonged—that is, seated at God's right hand—I could easily look down and see everything. From there I could determine three very important things. First, I could look back and see exactly

21

what had caused my problem. *Next,* I could *look down* and see where I was in relation to the solution of my problem. I could tell if I was moving toward the answer or away from it. *Best of all,* from that vantage point, *I could see what needed to be done to solve my problem.* From the right hand of God, I could intelligently speak to Him concerning my situation. From His throne, I could actually *direct the work of His hands.*

God Wants To Hear Your Advice

Please do not let the thought of telling God the solution to your problem upset you. Jesus Himself encouraged this kind of interaction between Himself and His disciples. When He was faced with feeding the multitude, He asked Philip how he thought the problem might be solved.

> **When Jesus then lifted up his eyes, and saw a great company come unto him, he saith unto Philip, Whence shall we buy bread, that these may eat? . . .**
> **John 6:5**

Since Philip did not have an answer, it was Andrew who was given the privilege of directing the hand of Jesus. Remember, it was Andrew who suggested using the little boy's lunch in the miracle.

> **One of his disciples, Andrew, Simon Peter's brother, saith unto him,**

> ***There is a lad here, which hath five barley loaves, and two small fishes. . . .***
>
> **And Jesus took the loaves; and when he had given thanks, he distributed to the disciples, and the disciples to them that were set down; and likewise of the fishes as much as they would."**
> **John 6:8,9,11**

That entire discourse was little more than a test to see if His disciples were ready to rule and reign with Him.

I Have Directed My Father's Hand

When I was a young man, I worked for my father. During that time, he directed every aspect of my schedule. He would give me a list of things to do each day.

Later on I became his superintendent in charge of building houses. As a superintendent, I no longer worked *for* him. He then expected me to work *with* him. That experience taught me that it is perfectly acceptable for a responsible son to direct the hand of his father. In fact, as I matured, my dad expected me to guide him to the solutions of many of his problems. Once I was superintendent, he no longer wanted to tell me everything that needed to be done. He actually took *delight* in seeing me take authority in my area of responsibility. He was so desirous of my guiding his hands that when I gave him proper solutions, he would *financially reward me.*

Considering my practical experience made it much easier for me to understand how it would please God to have His sons and daughters take more authority in spiritual matters.

Signs And Wonders Follow

As my study continued, I found that when the children of God worked *with Him,* signs and wonders would come forth and confirm the Word of God.

> ... these signs shall follow them that believe; In my name shall they cast out devils; they shall speak with new tongues;
>
> They shall take up serpents; and if they drink any deadly thing, it shall not hurt them; they shall lay hands on the sick, and they shall recover. ...
>
> ... They went forth, and preached every where, *the Lord working with them,* and *confirming the word with signs following.* Amen.
>
> **Mark 16:17,18,20**

No wonder signs and wonders are in such short supply in our day. It is because so few of God's children are actually working *with Him.* The truth is that ignorance of the Word has kept most Christians from actually rising up to be seated with Him in the place of rulership.

> [God] hath raised us up together, and made us sit together in heavenly places in Christ Jesus.
>
> **Ephesians 2:6**

On To The Next Step

Next I began to look through the Bible for people who had prayed for long periods of time without getting their prayers answered. I must admit that it was a difficult part of my study. Much is written about prayer in the Bible. There are numerous prayers by both men and women that were answered, but nowhere could I find a list of unanswered prayers from the Word of God.

A Breakthrough Discovery

After considerable searching, I finally found two examples of Old Testament women whose long-term prayers were not being answered: Hannah and the widow at Zarephath. They had something peculiar in common. They both did the same thing which instantly turned their unanswered prayers into answered prayers. When I found that similarity, I immediately realized I had made a breakthrough discovery.

Now every serious Bible student knows that when he makes that type of discovery, bold new answers are just around the corner. However, I must say that when I understood what those two women did to move the hand of God, I did not like what I had learned. It was totally opposite of what I wanted to hear. In fact, what they did actually upset me.

Thankfully, I had been learning some basic truth about God and His revelation. I had been realizing that He does not do things the way men do them. His ways are usually the exact opposite of what my ways would be. God's Word bears out this truth.

> *. . . my thoughts are not your thoughts, neither are your ways my ways,* **saith the Lord.**
> **Isaiah 55:8**

Throughout my Christian life, I have found that whenever God reveals something new to me, His new way is not at all like my way. In fact, the most important things I have learned from God were somewhat, or even a whole lot, uncomfortable for me at first.

My Thoughts About Salvation

For instance, God's method of salvation is totally opposite of what I would have considered a good way to save people. When I first heard about being washed in blood, it did not appeal to me at all. Even though I had previously received some teaching about the crucifixion, I must admit that I was not comfortable with the concept that a human sacrifice had to be made for my salvation. To put it plainly, God's method of redemption was not what I expected it to be. However, I had to change my thinking in order to receive the benefit of salvation from God.

I must say that since being saved, one of the most precious concepts I know anything about is God's way of saving me. I am truly blessed that He washed me in His blood. Why, just hearing the first few words of the song, "There is a fountain filled with blood," brings tears to my eyes. God's thoughts are not my thoughts.

My Thoughts About
The Filling Of The Holy Spirit

Being filled with the Holy Spirit seemed desirable to me from the day I was saved. However, I was less than excited with God's requirement of my speaking with other tongues as evidence of having His Spirit in fullness. Before being filled with the Holy Spirit, I thought unknown tongues sounded like pure gibberish. Besides that, I had been taught against speaking in tongues at the Bible college I attended.

After I decided that the filling of the Holy Spirit was for today, I struggled for almost six months before receiving my prayer language. As unattractive as that requirement seemed to me at the time, I had to change my mind about it before I could receive God's gift. Now I daily speak with other tongues. Once again I had to face the fact that *God's ways are not my ways.*

My Thinking About Healing

I thank God so much for the wonderful miracle of healing. I was most appreciative of it when God miraculously healed my wife of a life-threatening tumor. A while after she received that miracle, I became aware that her healing was the direct result of a horrible whipping Jesus had received.

. . . by [His] stripes ye were healed.
1 Peter 2:24

It put me out of my comfort zone when I realized Jesus had to be beaten almost to death so we could be healed. However, once I knew it was God's way, I had to change my thinking. Now I boldly lay my hands on the sick, telling them of the love of their God — a love that brought Him to the whipping post so they could rise from the sickbed. Oh, how true it is that His ways are not our ways!

My Thinking About Service

In the early days of my salvation I wanted to become a deacon or an elder of the Church. I must admit it was the prestige of those offices that attracted me. How surprised I was to find that in order for me to increase in stature in the Church, God expected me to decrease. I would have to become the servant of all if I wanted to be a leader. How foolish it sounded at first. It seemed only right that the leader should be honored and served, but that isn't God's way for leaders to come forth.

. . . whosoever will be great among you, let him be your minister;

And whosoever will be chief among you, let him be your servant:

Even as the Son of man came not to be ministered unto, but to minister, and to give his life a ransom for many.

Matthew 20:26-28

His thoughts and His ways are higher than ours.

By this time in my study I had received fresh insight about how to turn unanswered prayer into answered prayer. I must confess that the explanations I was finding in the Word of God were infinitely better than anything I had received from the commentaries. However, even though I had learned it was God's will for His children to command Him concerning the works of His hand, I still did not clearly understand how to get His hand directed to my friend's point of need.

The Answer Worked

I am happy to say that after just a short time of further study, God revealed to me exactly how to move His hand to the point of need. I immediately shared what I had learned with the church member who got me started on my journey. In turn, he put the principle to work in his life, and I was blessed to hear that God miraculously began to move in his situation. Before the end of six months, his prayer was totally answered. He later shared with me that he would never again approach God with a problem of great urgency without using the method of prayer I had shown him from the Word of God.

A New Prayer Power Emerges

With the conclusion of my study and my friend's report of success, my wife and I began to use this principle in our own prayers. The results have been extremely satisfying. As you move to the next chapter, keep in mind that God is no respecter of persons. What He has done for others, He will also do for you. He is eager for you to direct His hand to the solution of the problem in your life.

2

Hannah's New Prayer

... she vowed a vow, and said ... remember
me ....

1 Samuel 1:11

One of the first places my study took me was to
Samuel's mother, Hannah. She was the wife of a godly
man named Elkanah. I came to realize that Hannah
must have prayed for a long period of time without
receiving an answer from God. Her prayer request was
a simple one. She wanted to have a child.

Not much is said about Hannah in Scripture, however, everything said about her is positive. In all my
years of study, I have never read even one bad comment
about Hannah. Her godly life is irrefutable.

Hannah's husband loved and honored her. We are
told that he purposely made her share double that of
his other wife, Peninnah. As you carefully read God's
Word, you will find that Peninnah was Hannah's adver-
sary. She would openly make fun of her because of
Hannah's barren womb.

Elkanah tried every way he could to comfort Hannah. He even excused her from child bearing saying that he would take the place of sons in her life. Though it was a kind gesture on his part, Hannah steadfastly continued to long for children.

Hannah Was A Woman Of Prayer

Elkanah and his family faithfully served the Most High God. They made it a practice to go regularly to Shiloh at the appointed times of feasting to worship God. During those pilgrimages, Elkanah gave generously to God. He was also careful to make all the proper sacrifices.

Since Hannah was a part of his godly household, it only stands to reason that she was a woman who prayed. Because of her great desire to have a child, we know she must have been in constant prayer that she might conceive. No doubt she would rise very early every morning with a special prayer on her lips, "Oh, God, give me a son! Please, God, give your handmaiden a child." All through the day, as regularly as clockwork, she must have called out to the Lord for a child.

There can be little doubt that she faithfully asked for a child each day. Everyone in the house probably knew her prayer by heart. Even the neighbors must have been involved as she would no doubt ask them again and again to agree with her in this special request. All the angels of heaven knew the desire of Hannah's heart as they constantly heard her prayer for a son rise up to the throne of God. To put it bluntly, it seemed as if everyone in heaven and earth had heard her prayer — everyone except God.

Desperation Led to Violent Action

Hannah finally hit bottom. Scripture says her grief for a son finally brought her to the point where she could no longer eat. At the very moment that her pain seemed to be the worst, she made a radical change in the way she prayed. All of a sudden, she made a desperate attempt to move the hand of God.

Thank God for the circumstances that cause us to throw tradition to the wind! Those are the times when we *violently* leap into God's presence. It is then that we are able to take hold of the things that are rightfully ours.

Child of God, please don't be repulsed by the thought of violence in the Kingdom of God. It is always a violent leap in faith that brings relief when the worst is about to happen. The Word of God bears this out:

> **. . . the kingdom of heaven suffereth violence, and the violent take it by force.**
> **Matthew 11:12**

A *desperate plunge* into the arms of God brings His supply in the time of need.

Lepers Who Took Violent Action

Remember the four lepers who sat starving at the gates of Samaria (2 Kings 7)? The Syrians had encircled the city. The food and water supply was cut off. In the best of times their existence would have been meager to say the least. You must remember that in those days lepers ate the leftovers from the city. The ongoing siege of Samaria had brought the city to total famine. Even the garbage pails were empty. Everyone within the gates of the city was at the brink of starvation.

It seems as though it is always the desperate who dare to lunge violently for survival. Read what those lepers did:

> . . . there were four leprous men . . . and they said one to another, *Why sit we here until we die?*
>
> . . . let us fall unto the host of the Syrians: *if they save us alive, we shall live; and if they kill us, we shall but die.*
>
> And they rose up . . . to go unto the camp of the Syrians: and when they were come to the uttermost part of the camp of Syria, behold, *there was no man there.*
>
> And when these lepers came to the uttermost part of the camp, they went into one tent, and *did eat and drink, and carried thence silver, and gold, and raiment*, and went and hid it; and came again, entered into another tent, and carried thence also, and went and hid it.
>
> 2 Kings 7:3-5,8

Those men had run out of options. *Only a miracle could save them.* In desperation, one asked, "Why are we sitting until we die? Let's do something!" How eternally grateful they must have been for their violent action when they found themselves fully fed and rich beyond their wildest dreams.

An Unorthodox Prayer

In that same way, Hannah made a desperate move. She went to the altar of God and prayed a totally unorthodox prayer. What she prayed was nothing short of spiritual violence. Say what you may about it, but one thing is sure. It was a prayer that *moved the hand of God.* The Bible says her womb was opened.

> **And she *vowed a vow* and said, O Lord of hosts, if thou wilt indeed look on the affliction of thine handmaid, and *remember me,* and *not forget thine handmaid,* but wilt *give unto thine handmaid a man child,* then *I will give* him unto the Lord all the days of his life, and there shall no razor come upon his head.**
>
> **1 Samuel 1:11**

Her prayer was a theological nightmare. It would have brought quick censorship had it been heard by the commentators of her day. Even today a prayer like hers might be called heresy. If you notice, she was openly accusing God of forgetting her.

God Uses Reminders

I don't want to debate the issue of whether or not God ever forgets us, but I do know He chooses to use memory joggers. Don't take my word for it. Let me show you just a few of them from the Bible.

God Has Tattoos

> Behold, I have *graven thee* upon the palms of my hands. . . .
>
> **Isaiah 49:16**

Our names are tattooed inside His palms so that we are continually kept before Him. The context shows that it is to keep Him from forgetting us.

Stone Memorials Of Israel

> And thou shalt put the two stones upon the shoulders of the ephod for *stones of memorial* unto the children of Israel: and Aaron shall bear their names before the Lord upon his two shoulders *for a memorial.*
>
> **Exodus 28:12**

The priest wore stones representing the children of Israel upon his shoulders when he went before God. Think of it. God used stone memorials to remember Israel.

Moses Reminded God

And the Lord said unto Moses, I have seen this people, and, behold, it is a stiffnecked people:

Now therefore let me alone, that my wrath may wax hot against them, and that I may consume them: and I will make of thee a great nation.

And Moses besought the Lord his God, and said, Lord, why doth thy wrath wax hot against thy people, which thou has brought forth out of the land of Egypt with great power, and with a mighty hand?

Wherefore should the Egyptians speak, and say, For mischief did he bring them out, to slay them in the mountains, and to consume them from the face of the earth? Turn from thy fierce wrath, and repent of this evil against thy people.

Remember Abraham, Isaac, and Israel, thy servants, to whom thou swarest by thine own self, and saidst unto them, I will multiply your seed as the stars of heaven, and all this land that I have spoken of will I give unto your seed, and they shall inherit it for ever.

And the Lord repented of the evil which he thought to do unto his people.

Exodus 32:9-14

I hope that long passage of Scripture opens your eyes to something quite unique. God seems to react when His memory is jogged.

Hannah Demanded An Answer

No matter what the theologians thought, to Hannah her new way of praying did not seem to be heresy. She was actually asking some legitimate questions of her God. She was violently confronting Him with the *scandal of her unanswered prayer*. She was crying out as a *neglected* child, "Lord, please remember me. Whatever you do, don't forget me." She was storming the palace of God with her prayer. She was demanding an answer. She was doing everything she knew to focus God's attention on her unanswered request. To put it plainly, she was bargaining with God. If He would remember her and give her a child, she would give him back to God.

> *. . . if thou wilt . . . remember me, and not forget thine handmaid, but wilt give unto thine handmaid* a man child, then *I will give him unto the Lord* all the days of his life. . . .
>
> **1 Samuel 1:11**

My Education Was Offended

I must admit that when I read that verse, it did not sit well with me at all. Why, I had been to Bible college. I had studied at the seminary. Hannah's prayer was challenging everything the theologians had ever taught me.

Let's take a closer look at her prayer. Let's take it step by step to its answer.

First, she made a *vow.*
Secondly, she asked that God *no longer forget her.*
Finally, she *promised to give God a son* if he would open her womb.

At that point I thought, "She is offering God the pick of the litter!"

The trained mind would immediately say, "God would never answer a prayer like that!" The whole thing was theologically unsound. Hannah was breaking every rule of prayer I had ever heard. I had been taught to come to God empty handed, confessing my total unworthiness when I prayed. Yet here was a brazen, flagrant violation of that rule. Let's read the prayer one more time.

> **And she *vowed a vow,* and said, O Lord of hosts, if thou wilt indeed look on the affliction of thine handmaid, and *remember me,* and *not forget thine handmaid,* but wilt *give unto thine handmaid* a man child, then *I will give him unto the Lord* all the days of his life, and there shall no razor come upon his head.**
>
> **1 Samuel 1:11**

God Remembered

I would have quickly moved on to some other area of God's Word, but I noticed something amazing. Look with me at verse 19:

> **And they rose up in the morning early, and**
> **worshipped before the Lord, and returned, and**
> **came to their house to Ramah: and Elkanah knew**
> **Hannah his wife;** *and the Lord remembered her.*
> **1 Samuel 1:19**

There it was, plain as day! *God remembered her!* He answered her prayer! It happened in record time. As soon as they got home, the Bible says Elkanah knew his wife, and *the Lord remembered her.*

Please do not miss the significance of this. The verse that relates Hannah's prayer is nothing more than an accurate account of how she prayed. That does not mean she prayed correctly. However, when the Bible goes on to say God remembered her, that is something else. Holy Scripture is saying God answered her prayer. The fact that He says He remembered her should shut the mouth of the theologian and vindicate Hannah, making her method of prayer legitimate.

The proof goes beyond verse nineteen, for after Samuel was born, Hannah had several other children.

> **And the Lord visited Hannah, so that she con-**
> **ceived, and bare three sons and two daughters.**
> **And the child Samuel grew before the Lord.**
> **1 Samuel 2:21**

Let's Review

Let's take a quick review of what we have just learned. A godly woman prayed *unsuccessfully* for years for a son. Not one of her thousands of prayers concerning her desire was answered. Unanswered prayer brought her to the door of desperation. Finally, she went one more time to the altar of God. There she began her most effective prayer with a *vow* (a sincere promise). She boldly stated she felt God had forgotten her. She asked that she be forgotten no longer. She wanted to be remembered. She offered what the unlearned might call a bribe. She promised to give to God if He would remember her and not forget her.

Her boldness is clearly seen when she made her gift conditional. Before she could give the gift, God would have to answer her prayer.

> . . . if thou wilt . . . give unto thine handmaid a man child, *then* I will give him unto the Lord all the days of his life. . . .
>
> 1 Samuel 1:11

It cannot be ignored. With her *new method of praying,* she received her answer within days. Once Samuel was weaned, she delivered what she had promised to God, and He honored her by giving her six more children. Read Hannah's own words:

> They that were full have hired out themselves for bread; and they that were hungry ceased: so that *the barren hath borne seven.* . . .
>
> 1 Samuel 2:5

This Might Be A Coincidence

Surely this method of praying could not be an acceptable pattern for prayer. The fact that her womb was opened has to be a coincidence. However, if it is not a coincidence, most of our prayer theology will have to be rewritten.

Please don't let this insight turn you off. Read again the key verse to receiving revelation from God.

> **For my thoughts are not your thoughts, neither are your ways my ways, saith the Lord. For as the heavens are higher than the earth, so are my ways higher than your ways, and my thoughts than your thoughts.**
> **Isaiah 55:8,9**

Remember, *God's ways and thoughts are higher than ours*. Focus your thoughts on God's superior mentality.

> **O the depth of the riches both of the wisdom and knowledge of God!** *How unsearchable are his judgments, and his ways past finding out!*
> **Romans 11:33**

Revelation, Not Investigation

That verse explains why most theologians find their systematized answers in opposition with the plain truth of God's Word. They reach their conclusions about God solely by investigation. Investigation will unlock the secrets of science and nature, but it will not work in determining the thoughts and ways of God. His ways are *past finding out* (beyond investigation).

Then how will we ever know the mind of God? How could Moses have known the ways of God?

> He made known his *ways* unto Moses, his *acts* unto the children of Israel.
>
> **Psalm 103:7**

The *method of knowing God's ways* will be confusing to you unless you understand something the Apostle Paul told us.

> . . . we speak *the wisdom of God in a mystery,* even the *hidden wisdom,* which God ordained before the world unto our glory:
>
> Which *none of the princes of this world knew:* for had they known it, they would not have crucified the Lord of glory.
>
> But as it is written, *Eye* hath not seen, nor *ear* heard, neither have entered into the *heart* of man, the things which God hath prepared for them that love him.
>
> But God hath *revealed* them unto us *by his Spirit:* for the Spirit searcheth all things, yea, the deep things of God.
>
> For what man knoweth the things of a man, save the spirit of man which is in him? even so *the things of God knoweth no man, but the Spirit of God.*
>
> Now we have received, *not the spirit of the world* [investigation and reason], but *the spirit*

which is of God [revelation]; *that we might know* the things that are freely given to us of God.

Which things also we speak, *not in the words which man's wisdom teacheth*, but which the *Holy Ghost teacheth;* comparing spiritual things with spiritual.

But the *natural man receiveth not the things of the Spirit of God* [revelation]: for they are foolishness unto him: *neither can he know them,* because they are spiritually discerned [spiritually revealed].

But he that is spiritual judgeth [understands] all things, yet he himself is judged [understood] of no man.

For who hath known the mind of the Lord, *that he may instruct him? But we have the mind of Christ.*
1 Corinthians 2:7-16

Paul said we speak the *hidden* wisdom of God. That is the kind of wisdom that cannot be found out by *investigation.* Neither can it be discovered by the five senses (verse 9). It cannot be perceived by the processes of the natural mind. The method by which we can know the things of God is by *revelation from the Spirit of God* (verse 10). *We know all things!*

Comparing Spiritual Things With Spiritual Things

Don't get the idea that Paul was teaching us to abandon the constant investigation of the Scripture. Heaven forbid! In fact, he was encouraging it. He said we should continually compare spiritual things with the

Scripture (spiritual things). The main emphasis is that revelation does not come from *human conclusions*. It comes by *divine illumination through the power of the Holy Spirit.*

Paul Said We Should Instruct God

Notice how Paul confirmed the thought of Isaiah 45:11, ". . . concerning the work of my hands command ye me." Look at verse 16 again.

> **For who hath known the mind of the Lord, that he may instruct him?** *But we have the mind of Christ.*
> **1 Corinthians 2:16**

When we know the mind of Christ, we become qualified for Isaiah 45:11:

> **. . . concerning the work of my hands command ye me.**
> **Isaiah 45:11**

With this in mind, we see how important Hannah's prayer is to those who need an answer from God.

Drop Tradition

What I am teaching you is not only important because it moved the hand of God to open Hannah's womb. It is also important because *it will help you move God's hand to the needs in your life.* What you are learning rejects *traditional prayer* and puts *effective biblical prayer* in its place. It bypasses the satisfaction of man's instruction and reaches beyond to the satisfaction of man's need.

Prayer And Giving Mixed

When Hannah *mingled* her prayers with her giving, God moved rapidly on her behalf. In the following chapter you will see how this same method worked for a widow who was in great need.

Please keep this in mind. If you ever hope to move into the revelation of this book, you must be convinced that God has better thoughts and ways for us to communicate with Him than men do, for His thoughts are higher than our natural thoughts.

> . . . my thoughts *are not* your thoughts, *neither* are your ways my ways, saith the Lord. For as the heavens are higher than the earth, *so are my ways higher than your ways,* and my thoughts than your thoughts.
>
> **Isaiah 55:8,9**

If you now have a firm hold on that verse, you are ready to proceed to chapter 3. While reading this book, if at any time its concept begins to overwhelm you, just refer back to this special passage (Isaiah 55:8,9). It will tend to stabilize you.

3

A Widow Moved
The Hand Of God

. . . make me thereof a little cake first. . . .

**And she went and did according to the saying
of Elijah. . . .**

And the barrel of meal wasted not. . . .
1 Kings 17:13,15,16

My attention was next drawn to a woman who was
just hours from disaster when the prophet gave her the
word that showed her how to move the hand of God.
Like Hannah, she was a godly woman. From a close
examination of the Scripture, we must conclude that
she prayed often over her diminishing supply of meal
and oil. When Elijah appeared at her house, she was
only one meal away from death by starvation.

Only One Widow Moved God's Hand

It is important to understand exactly how this widow
prayed, for her prayer was unlike any other of her day.
It was a starvation-breaking prayer. Jesus said she was
the only widow who moved God's hand in that famine.

> But I tell you of a truth, *many widows* were in Israel in the days of Elias, when the heaven was shut up three years and six months, when great famine was throughout all the land;
>
> But unto none of them was Elias sent, save unto Sarepta, a city of Sidon, unto a woman that was a widow.
>
> Luke 4:25,26

That verse should get the attention of every born-again Christian. A widow formed such a powerful prayer that God answered her while every other widow's prayer went unanswered.

Let's Learn What We Can About Her

All Christians should know some important things about this widow. First, we must realize that she was, without a doubt, *one of the most spiritual women mentioned in the Old Testament.* Let me go even further and say I believe she was *one of the most spiritual women who ever lived.* That may sound like a presumptuous statement, especially if you are familiar with her story. However, before her spiritual fiber can be judged, we must go back to the first mention of her in the Bible.

> . . . behold, I have *commanded* a widow woman there to sustain thee.
>
> 1 Kings 17:9

There we see the widow as she really was. She was a woman who walked so closely to God that He *manifested* Himself to her. He spoke to her in an *audible* voice and commanded her to feed His prophet, Elijah. Few women of the Bible have had that level of encounter with God.

Unfortunately her fame has not come from her walk with God but from her refusal at first to give Elijah a bite to eat. I realize that for a brief moment her fear caused her to refuse to do what God had commanded her, but don't forget that even the great Elijah was just a few days away from being so full of fear he would run away from Jezebel (1 Kings 19:1-4).

God forgive us for remembering this widow for the worst minute of her life instead of her best. There is no doubt about it. She had been a great witness for the Lord. There is little question that she had been God's powerhouse at Zarephath. She was in such close fellowship with her God that on at least one occasion, He spoke *audibly* to her.

Responsibilities Of A Single Mother

Having established the godliness of this woman, let's look more closely at the circumstances that brought her and her son to the brink of starvation. Take into consideration that there was a harsh famine in progress. Also keep in mind that she was a widow. She had no husband to help her meet expenses. To add to her hardship, women of her day were not able to find high-paying jobs. Then, to complicate her situation even further, she had a dependent son. She had to supply not only for her own needs, but for the needs of a growing boy as well.

I would venture to say that most of my readers could not tell me the exact number of meals that remain in their cupboards. Some might approximate, but most have no exact knowledge. However, there are some readers who could probably give me an exact inventory, even down to the last crumb in the bread box. The unique folks I speak of are *the single mothers* — those women in our midst who are raising children without a father in the house. The next time you meet one of those dear women, ask her about her cupboard. She will probably be able to tell you right down to the number of crackers hidden on the back shelf.

It Was Not Her First Prayer

This single mother was no different. She knew she had only one meal left. I am convinced that her prayers did not begin on the day the measuring cup scraped the bottom of the barrel. No doubt, she had repeatedly prayed to God about her dwindling supply. Night and day her petitions went up to God. Can't you just hear her pray, "Oh, Lord, my son and I need a miracle. If you don't help us, we will surely perish! Lord, have you forgotten us? If you will not do it for my sake, please do it for my little boy."

Hers was a legitimate prayer request. There is nothing wrong with asking God for enough to eat. Jesus even taught us to do this:

Give us this day our daily bread.
Matthew 6:11

Notice that absolutely nothing had happened as she prayed. Every day things just continued to go from bad to worse. Then one horrible day it was almost over. The last cup of meal was all she had left. The eleventh hour had come, and God had not moved. The death angel stood at the door. As the widow realized that she and her son were about to die, fear gripped her heart. It was a most devastating fear, *the fear of insufficiency!*

Her Son's Last Meal
Was Just Too Much To Ask

Maybe the dear woman could have fended off the fear of insufficiency if God's command had involved giving up only her own last meal. However, it was not just her food that was being required, but it was also the food of her precious child.

No doubt she had been watching the distant horizon for many days. She knew the prophet was on his way. If only he had come when the barrel was half full. It would have been so much easier to give out of a half-full barrel. Why, even if it was one-third full it could have been done. But now the barrel was empty except for the one meager handful that remained.

The day of the last meal had arrived. On that dreadful morning she was gathering a few small sticks that would provide the fire for the last meal she would ever prepare. All of a sudden her eyes saw the figure of the prophet Elijah coming toward her. Without hesitation he was heading straight to her door.

You must remember, this was the same woman who had spoken face to face with God. It would not have been proper for Elijah to visit any home until he had visited hers. Not only that, but by now the pangs of hunger were surely biting into his belly, and she was the one God said would feed him.

She Said "Yes" To A Cup Of Water

To relieve the dryness in his throat, the prophet began by asking her for a drink of water. Without hesitation she moved to fetch it. Notice that with all that was within her, she attempted to obey the request of the man of God.

Even as she moved to get the water, she silently dreaded the moment she knew would come. She knew in her heart that sooner or later Elijah would ask for some food. God had told her he would.

As she hastened to get the water, she heard the words she feared most. *"Bring me a morsel of bread."* Elijah could have asked for almost anything else, and she would have gladly given it to him. He could have asked for a chair to sit on, a change of clothing, or even a blanket to ward off the evening chill. He could have asked for a place to rest from his journey — anything except *something to eat,* for her barrel of supply was now empty.

Unanswered Prayer Can Break Your Faith

Only then did the disappointment of hundreds of unanswered prayers become fully evident. She had not prayed selfishly. She had known for some time Elijah was coming. She knew that more than her own family would be eating from the barrel of meal. She had faithfully prayed that there would be more than enough — not only enough for her own needs, but plenty extra so the man of God could eat until he was full.

How hard it is when our prayers for finances and supply go unanswered. The moment that should have been her happiest was now becoming her worst, for the man of God was asking for her last bite. Observe how unanswered prayer had broken this good woman's faith.

> . . . **As the Lord** *thy* **God liveth, I have not a cake, but an handful of meal in a barrel, and a little oil in a cruse. . . .**
> **1 Kings 17:12**

Notice she did not say, "as the Lord *my* God liveth," but "as the Lord *thy* God liveth." Don't you know that mixed emotions caused her to question the prophet's reputation? She must have wondered how he could be a prophet and not know about her short supply. Maybe he did know, and he just didn't care.

Her once strong faith was broken, for she no longer referred to God as *her God,* but now God was *the prophet's God.*

Deadlines Have Come And Gone In My Life

The woman's answer to Elijah's request has always sent a chill down my spine. It brings to my remembrance the times I stood with my family, facing the eleventh hour of need. We had prayed. We had patiently waited for an answer only to see the deadline come and go without God's supply.

Maybe we now understand the widow better. When God does not seem to be answering prayer, there is sometimes a tendency to give up on life itself! But don't count her out yet. Remember, she had lived most of her life as a woman of faith, and there was a man of God who cared for her soul.

Fear Not

Now, pay close attention to how Elijah ministered to her. He gave her two great words of instruction. First, he *cut off* her connection with unbelief. He said, *"Fear not!"* (1 Kings 17:13).

Oh, child of God. If we could only learn that fear is the pipeline that runs from the kingdom of darkness into the hearts of men. Fear can literally turn a child of God into a negative magnet. It will draw to you everything that is contrary to your best interest. The Book of Job gives a word of warning about fear.

> . . . the thing which *I greatly feared* is come upon me, and *that which I was afraid of* is come unto me.
>
> **Job 3:25**

Job told us it was fear that drew into his life all those terrible things that came upon him. His own fear ushered in total poverty and sickness. In that state, even Job had to spend some time begging for his daily bread.

Remember, when fear comes upon you, *it has not come from God.*

> For God *hath not* given us the *spirit* of fear; but of power, and of love, and of a sound mind.
>
> **2 Timothy 1:7**

The worst thing you can do in the time of insufficiency is to allow fear to enter your heart. It will only speed up the thing you are desperately trying to avoid.

I thank God that this woman at Zarephath knew a man of God she could trust. If Elijah had not lived a godly life before her, I doubt that he would have been able to minister to her. If his life had been full of sin or inconsistencies, she would not have been able to believe him. Even though she temporarily doubted God, suddenly the prophet's words of ministry began to work in her heart.

Trust Your Man Of God

The devil knows what will stop your miracle supply. He has an effective campaign in full swing to discredit the men and women of God. It is a calculated and deliberate plan to block the prosperity of God's children. Satan knows that when the day comes that Christians walk in full prosperity, his kingdom will be doomed. For when the Church lives in abundance, it will not take long to totally evangelize the world. For that reason, the devil wants the children of God to doubt their leaders. Yes, that's right. Distrusting Christian leaders blocks prosperity.

> . . . Believe in the Lord your God, so shall ye be established; *believe his prophets, so shall ye prosper.*
>
> **2 Chronicles 20:20**

Not believing in the honesty of God's men and women holds the majority of Christians outside God's full financial blessings.

Notice how critical it was to the widow and her son that she could believe her man of God. She had to make a life-and-death decision. If she had thought Elijah wanted only what he could get from her, she would not have been able to give him the last bite of food she had. But with just a few reassuring words from him, the widow defeated fear and quickly rose into the realm of strong faith—faith that totally turned the devil's program around and placed her and her son in abundance for many months.

Watch Your Mouth

Elijah's second instruction was equally as important.

> . . . *go and do as thou hast said.* . . .
> **1 Kings 17:13**

Exactly what had the woman said just prior to Elijah's instructions? She had said she and her son were going to eat.

How very important the prophet's words were! If she ignored them and continued to speak of death and insufficiency, God could not work the miracle of increase she so desperately needed. When it is time to give, never forget the following words that Jesus spoke:

> . . . **whosoever shall** *say* **unto this mountain, Be thou removed, and be thou cast into the sea; and** *shall not doubt in his heart,* **but** *shall believe* **that those things** *which he saith* **shall come to pass;** *he shall have whatsoever he saith.*
> **Mark 11:23**

You will have *whatever you say.* If you say, "Mountain, be removed," and you do not doubt, the mountain will have to move out of your way.

There has been much negative response to what is called the teaching of "positive confession." Even though many criticize it, that does not diminish its truth. As we all know, we do not interpret the Bible by popular vote. It is interpreted by what it says, and Jesus said *you will have what you say.*

The man of God confirmed that the widow's plan to eat a meal was a good one. He told her to go right ahead with that plan.

> . . . go and do as thou hast said. . . .
> 1 Kings 17:13

She Added Giving To Praying

Notice that she lacked only one thing to move the hand of God into that barrel of meal. The praying had already been done. The man of God told her what was missing. *She had to add giving to her prayer.*

> . . . make me thereof a little cake first. . . .
> 1 Kings 17:13

Child of God, allow this to get into your spirit. When the man of God appears in your life, even if he comes with an offering plate in his hand, he has not been sent to spoil your picnic. Giving is an essential part of effective prayer. Notice this most familiar verse of Scripture from the lips of our Lord Jesus that conveys the same principle:

> *Give, and it shall be given unto you;* good measure, pressed down, and shaken together, and running over, shall men give into your bosom. For

with the same measure that ye mete withal it shall be measured to you again.
Luke 6:38

Elijah's ministry to the woman gave her the missing ingredient she needed to direct God's hand into her empty meal barrel. He boldly told her to add *giving* to her *praying.* He openly promised her that if she gave, she would *move the hand of God.*

. . . make me thereof a little cake first. . . .

For thus saith the Lord God of Israel, *The barrel of meal shall not waste, neither shall the cruse of oil fail,* **until the day that the Lord sendeth rain upon the earth.**
1 Kings 17:13,14

Now we can see the true spirit of this great woman. After just a few words from her man of God, her negative death wish was turned into enough faith power to command the hand of God into her food supply.

And she went and did according to the saying of Elijah: and *she, and he, and her house, did eat many days.*
1 Kings 17:15

There is no doubt about it. When she gave Elijah the cake, she added the missing ingredient to her unanswered prayer. She *gave to God* in a most special way. *She gave the last thing she had!* How thankful she must have been that her man of God knew enough about God's Word to tell her how to avert the death angel!

And the barrel of meal wasted not, neither did the cruse of oil fail, according to the word of the Lord, which he spake by Elijah.
1 Kings 17:16

In The Mouth Of Two Witnesses

There you have another example of sincere prayer without results. Then suddenly, when *giving* was mixed with the *prayer,* the hand of God swiftly moved to meet the need of His dear child. It happened to *Hannah,* and now we see that it happened to the *widow at Zarephath.* These two cases confirm the principle I am teaching, and according to the Word of God, two confirmations are enough.

. . . In the mouth of two or three witnesses shall every word be established.
2 Corinthians 13:1

Two witnesses are enough, but praise God! This great truth is found *in more than just these two places in God's Word.* It repeats itself again and again throughout the Bible, in the Old and New Testaments. It has also repeated itself daily in my life and in the lives of many others. Every day more and more people are learning to move God's hand by mixing their prayers with their giving.

With each additional illustration of this truth, whether it be from Scripture or from personal testimony, your faith in the effectiveness of this kind of prayer will grow. Your ability to implement it into your own life will increase with each chapter.

Next we will see how another great life-or-death victory was won when a mighty man of God used this same kind of prayer to direct God's hand against his enemies.

4

Jephthah's Emergency Prayer

. . . If thou shalt . . . deliver the children of
Ammon into mine hands,

Then it shall be that whatsoever cometh forth
of the doors of my house . . . I will offer it. . . .

Judges 11:30,31

Imagine how you would feel if God chose you to lead
His army into a real shooting war. Then, in the midst
of the battle, you suddenly realized that the enemy God
had sent you to destroy was about to destroy you. That
is actually what happened to a man called Jephthah.

Off To A Bad Start

Jephthah was one of those men who was personally
acquainted with disappointment. His father had never
married his mother, who was a prostitute by profession.
On top of that, Jephthah's half brothers ran him out of
town. To add insult to injury, they refused to give him
his share of his father's estate. It seemed everything
that could go wrong in Jephthah's life had gone wrong.

The Toughening Process

No doubt he was hurt, discouraged, and angry about all his misfortune, but sometimes it is only after men have thoroughly disappointed us that God can really begin to use us.

With no stretch of the imagination could Jephthah be considered to be a choice relative. As an illegitimate son of a harlot, he was never the favorite visitor to his family reunions. However, when people are treated shamefully, they seem to toughen up. The things he experienced in growing up strengthened him and developed him into a fighter.

During Jephthah's exile, an old enemy of Israel decided to go to war against them. Suddenly Jephthah became valuable to his countrymen. They realized he was the best qualified to lead them into battle against Ammon. A delegation was sent to the city of Tob to ask him to come home and lead the army of God against the pending danger.

From Outcast To Leader

The Bible says that Jephthah accepted the invitation, and as it is so many times, the underdog became the leader. With war pending, he followed the standard procedure in building his army. As was the custom, he marched through Israel gathering recruits as he traveled to the battlefront. His movements took him and his army in an easterly direction. His recruitment process began in the land of Manasseh, then he crossed the River Jordan near Gilead. When he had raised his army, he traveled on into the land of Ammon to face Israel's enemy.

Now, please keep in mind that this great adventure was not Jephthah's idea. It was clearly the instruction of Jehovah God for him to follow this orderly process of building the army.

> *Then the Spirit of the Lord came upon Jephthah,* **and he passed over Gilead, and Manasseh, and passed over Mizpeh of Gilead, and from Mizpeh of Gilead he passed over unto the children of Ammon.**
>
> **Judges 11:29**

The Holy Spirit was upon Jephthah as God led him and the army of Israel into battle.

Betrayed By Brothers

While the scriptural account is not detailed as to exactly what happened, it is clear that some part of the plan went very wrong. The cause of the problem would be unknown except for a portion of Scripture in chapter twelve. It reveals that one of the tribes of Israel did not come to Jephthah's assistance when he called them. It is evident that when it was time for them to move into the battle with Israel, the tribe of Ephraim refused to help.

> . . . when I called you, *ye delivered me not* out
> of their hands.
>
> Judges 12:2

That lack of support on Ephraim's part put the army of Israel at great peril. The balance of power drastically shifted to Ammon. All of a sudden, Jephthah and the army of God faced the grim reality that without God's intervention, they would be defeated.

When Time Is Of The Essence

When the enemy comes in like a flood, time becomes very important. With only moments to spare, Jephthah had to move the hand of God quickly into the battle or all would be lost. Hear how this great leader of Israel prayed when *immediate* action was needed.

> And Jephthah *vowed a vow unto the Lord.* . . .
> Judges 11:30

Keep in mind that those were not the words of a modern-day fund raiser. Jephthah was not the keynote speaker at a building fund banquet. They were the words of prayer spoken by a desperate man on a real battlefield with death just a few moments away.

The Most Effective Prayer Was Chosen

Of all the many kinds of prayer Jephthah might have used, he chose to use prayer mixed with giving to move the hand of God. His vow was clear and concise.

> **And Jephthah** *vowed a vow unto the Lord,* **and said,** *If thou shalt without fail deliver the children of Ammon into mine hands,*
>
> **Then it shall be, that** *whatsoever cometh forth of the doors of my house* **to meet me, when I return in peace from the children of Ammon,** *shall surely be the Lord's,* **and I will offer it up for a burnt offering.**
>
> **Judges 11:30,31**

Jephthah could have worded his prayer in a hundred different ways. Strange as it may seem, he did not use any of the popular methods of praying. Instead, he chose to mingle a gift with his prayer.

I am convinced he was not experimenting. It surely was not the time or place to test some hearsay prayer method. He had only a few precious minutes to form his prayer. It had to be one that would move the hand of God. If he missed, all Israel would be defeated. As the armies of Ammon were breaking through his first lines of defense, Jephthah had to use the type of prayer that he knew would bring an instant result.

The Most Liberal Offering Possible Was Given

Notice the quality of the offering he made. "Whatever comes out of my house first shall be yours, Lord." Jephthah's offering was among the most liberal that is possible. With his prayer he actually opened the entire inventory of his possessions to God. Surely God had the power to bring forth whatever He wanted from the house.

Now, let's see if his prayer worked.

> So Jephthah passed over unto the children of
> Ammon to fight against them; and *the Lord
> delivered them into his hands.*
> **Judges 11:32**

A Three-fold Cord Is Not Soon Broken

With the account of Jephthah's prayer, we now have before us three powerful cases of giving and praying being mixed together. First we read of the great gift Hannah mixed with her prayer. It quickly moved God's hand to open her womb. Secondly, we studied the life-saving prayer and gift of the widow of Zarephath. It moved the hand of God into her empty meal barrel. Thirdly, we have Jephthah, a man who was deserted by his comrades (Ephraim) and left to be slaughtered by the Ammonites. When he mixed his praying and giving together, immediately God's hand moved into the battle and helped him defeat the heathen army of Ammon.

Let The Word Of God Override Traditions

If you will let the clear message of these verses override the traditions of men, you will find that this ancient biblical method of praying is not a coincidence. By the time you have seen a few more examples from Scripture, you should be convinced that mixing your prayers with your gifts is a Bible-centered, God-honored method for receiving answers to urgent needs.

There is no doubt that you can command the work of God's hands.

> ... concerning the work of my hands command ye me.
>
> **Isaiah 45:11**

A Mistranslation Damaged Jephthah's Reputation

I must interject something at this point. All of Jephthah's problems did not come from his half brothers. Neither did they all come from Ammon, nor even from the cowardly tribe of Ephraim. Considerable damage has been done to his reputation by none other than the King James translators. They mistakenly translated a word in such a way that it sounds as if Jephthah offered his own daughter to the Lord as a human sacrifice. Unfortunately, this error has reduced the Church's exposure to this great man of God. It has actually caused his name to be almost forgotten among Christians.

It is totally out of the spirit of the context to believe Jephthah offered his daughter as a burnt offering. That is in no way in agreement with what we know about Jephthah or what we know about Jehovah God. The greatest evidence of that fact is our knowledge that the Holy Spirit would not have delivered Israel in order to receive a human sacrifice. Our God would have nothing to do with such a gift!

Before going on to the next chapter, I would like to offer an explanation of the words *burnt offering* from the King James translation.

Strong's concordance gives a different definition from that of the King James translators. The word *burnt* is the Hebrew word *owlah*. James Strong defines it as "a step or (stairs, as ascending); usually [but not always] a holocaust (as going up in smoke)."

The *King James Version* translated *owlah* three different ways: "ascent," "burnt offering (sacrifice)," or "go up to." The word *offering* as used in this verse does not even appear in the original text. It was added by the King James writers.

Jephthah promised God that whatever first came from his house would be given to the Lord. He simply said he would deliver it to God on the "ascent" or on the way up to the altar. The word *altar* is implied because that is where people always placed things given to God.

Jephthah's Daughter

We all know who came out the door first. It was Jephthah's only child, a precious daughter. Most people don't realize the true significance of that gift, for they are distracted by the erroneous translation of the *King James Version.*

The reason Jephthah tore his clothes in grief when he saw his daughter come out of the house first was that it meant she would never bear children. Remember, she was his only child. If she never bore him grandchildren, his lineage would be cut off from the earth.

That she would never have children is evident from the fact that she went from one end of Israel to the other *bemoaning her virginity.* Doesn't it seem strange that she grieved only over her virginity, and did not bemoan her impending death?

Jephthah Kept His Promise To God

A promise to God is a promise that must be kept. At the end of two months, her father took her to the altar where she began to serve God, remaining a virgin all the days of her life.

> And it came to pass at the end of two months, that she returned unto her father, who did with her according to his vow which he had vowed: and she knew no man. And it was a custom in Israel,
>
> That the daughters of Israel went yearly to lament the daughter of Jephthah the Gileadite four days in a year.
>
> **Judges 11:39,40**

Women Were Also Nazarites

Some would ask, "How can that be? What would a woman do at the altar?"

71

Why, she would become a Nazarite! The qualifications are found in the Book of Numbers. A Nazarite was a special person in Israel who was totally dedicated to the Lord and to His service. The requirements were very stringent and called for a chaste life. Scripture plainly states that *either a man or a woman could function in the office of a Nazarite!*

> . . . either *man or woman* shall separate them-
> selves to vow a vow of a Nazarite, to separate
> themselves unto the Lord. . . .
> **Numbers 6:2**

I believe Jephthah presented his daughter as a female Nazarite. Because of the Nazarite vow and vow of virginity, she would never have children. That is why people mourned her.

> . . . she knew no man. . . .
> **Judges 11:39**

I hope these few words have helped you more clearly understand the mistranslation. However, my purpose in writing this book is not to correct the King James translation. It is to show you a powerful way to move the hand of God wherever you need it to be.

We must definitely add Jephthah to our list of godly men and women who effectively mixed their giving with their prayers to *move the hand of God.*

5

A Roman Soldier Built A Memorial

> . . . Thy prayers and thine alms are come up for a memorial before God.
>
> **Acts 10:4**

What you are about to read will continue to give a biblical basis for the material I have already presented. After this chapter, there will no longer be any way to deny what you have read. The Bible will have established that mixing your prayers with your offerings effectively moves the hand of God.

At this time I would like to introduce you to the key figure in this teaching. Everything the Bible says about him is found in the Book of Acts. Although the information given is limited, it is explicit. You will find that he was one of the most important characters in the entire New Testament. The man I refer to is the Roman soldier named Cornelius.

A Gentile Who Loved God

The Bible tells us Cornelius held the rank of a centurion in a Roman military unit called the Italian band. He was a Gentile by birth. Until the account about him appeared in Scripture, it looked as if salvation was going to be exclusively for the Jews.

Then Simon Peter received a rooftop visit from God. In a vision God told him the Gentiles were ready for the gospel. After that revelation, Cornelius immediately invited Simon Peter to Caesarea to visit him and those of his household.

A Faithful Gentile

Scripture tells us that Cornelius was a devout man, one who eagerly sought a relationship with Jehovah God. Not only did he seek the truth, but he faithfully put into practice the truth he had learned. He willingly gave of his money to the poor. His relationship with God went beyond giving, for he also was a man of diligent prayer.

Don't make the mistake of missing how special Cornelius really was, for, remember, it was not common for Gentiles of his day to seek after the true and living God. He was a unique individual to say the least, for he played a key role in changing the history of the world. Every Gentile Christian owes him a debt of thanks for what he did, because when he found the way to move the hand of God, he opened the door of salvation to the entire world.

He Broke Tradition

Please keep in mind that it was not customary for a Jew to visit the home of a Gentile. However, you must remember that Cornelius was not just any Gentile. He was the Gentile *who got God's attention!* As he called to God for help, God called to Simon Peter to go help him.

Little did either of them know the eternal significance of their pending visit. Surely if the devil had known, he would have tried everything in his power to stop them from meeting.

As soon as Simon Peter stood before him, Cornelius explained why he had sent for him.

> . . . **Four days ago I was fasting until this hour; and at the ninth hour I prayed in my house, and, behold, a man stood before me in bright clothing,**
>
> **And said, Cornelius, *thy prayer is heard, and thine alms are had in remembrance in the sight of God.***
>
> **Acts 10:30,31**

Praying And Giving Mixed

Look closely at the words spoken by the heavenly messenger. "Your *prayer* and your *alms* [giving] *are had* in remembrance in the sight of God." These are important words. They show that when Cornelius mixed his prayers with his giving, both were strengthened. Together they formed something greater than either of them were alone. What I am trying to say is best said in mathematical terms: "*The sum is always greater than its parts.*"

He Formed A Perpetual Reminder

Prayer is great and powerful by itself. Giving is also very powerful. However, *when those two powers are linked together* in the way we have seen them linked in the first five chapters of this book, *they become even greater.* The Bible says they become an *ongoing reminder that lingers in the sight of God.*

> . . . thy prayer is heard, and thine alms *are had in remembrance* in the *sight* of God.
> Acts 10:31

This is an interesting series of words, *are had in remembrance.* Those words are the *present progressive form of the verb.* When your prayer is lifted to that tense, it literally takes on a *perpetual form.* When prayers are mixed with giving, those prayers take up *permanent residence* in the sight of God.

Please take time to digest that thought, for when its full impact hits you, *your prayer life will never be the same again.*

Look now at the next verse.

> *Send therefore* **to Joppa, and call hither Simon, whose surname is Peter. . . .**
> **Acts 10:32**

"Send therefore." Why was Cornelius given permission to send for Simon Peter? It was because of his faithful prayers mingled with his giving. The angel said, "Your *prayers* mingled with your *gifts* have placed your request in perpetual remembrance before God. Because of that, you may send for Simon Peter."

That statement clarifies what we have been studying in the previous chapters. It shows us that prayer mixed with giving strengthens and prolongs the effect of prayer. The fact that it influences the actions of God is clearly seen, for in this instance it brought a mighty man of God to the door of Cornelius the Gentile.

Our prayers and our offerings, when mixed together, form something more substantial than prayers or offerings alone.

Revelation Is Progressive

For several years that is all the revelation I had on this subject. While it was not perfect or complete, it worked. The hand of God was quickly moving when Pat and I mixed our prayers and our gifts together. Not only was it working for us, but it was bringing results to all those with whom I had shared it.

Even with all of the foregoing evidence, some may still not be convinced that what I am proposing is a biblical truth. I thank God for the irrefutable revelation I received when I realized what the first part of Acts 10 said about this method of prayer. With the following verses added to what we already know, the truth that prayers and offerings together bring greater results becomes conclusive.

> There was a certain man in Caesarea called Cornelius, a centurion of the band called the Italian band,
>
> A *devout man,* and one that *feared God* with all his house, which *gave much alms to the people, and prayed to God alway.*
>
> He saw in a vision evidently about the ninth hour of the day an angel of God coming in to him, and saying unto him, Cornelius.
>
> And when he looked on him, he was afraid, and said, What is it, Lord? And he said unto him, *Thy prayers and thine alms are come up for a memorial before God.*
>
> And now send men to Joppa, and call for one Simon, whose surname is Peter.
>
> Acts 10:1-5

Building A Memorial Prayer

Are you understanding the Word of the Lord? Cornelius was doing something bigger than giving. He was doing something bigger than praying. He was mixing the two into what *the Word of God* chooses to call *a memorial!*

Imagine, if you will, a stone of remembrance rising up before God, and on it, in permanent form, is your prayer! When we mix our prayers and our giving together, the Bible says we build *a memorial.*

> . . . **Thy prayers and thine alms are come up for a memorial before God.**
> **Acts 10:4**

The Word of God is not describing some dead memorial, like a tombstone. It is talking about something that is living. When we form a memorial prayer, we don't just word a prayer or just give a financial gift. We mingle the two together to build a living, self-perpetuating petition that remains in the sight of God until it is answered.

An Example From My Youth

When I was a young man, I worked as a brick layer. In that trade there is a cement-like substance called "mortar" that is placed between the bricks to hold them together.

Mortar has a special composition. It must be prepared in a particular way. It begins as a dry powder that must be thoroughly mixed with water. If you put the powdered mortar between the bricks without the water, the wind will blow it away. If you put the water between the bricks without the powdered mortar, it will evaporate. But when you properly mix the powdered mortar with the water, it becomes as hard as cement. It takes on a perpetual form. It stays between the bricks as long as the wall stands.

I have personally laid the brick in many walls that are now over thirty years old, and the mortar is still in place. In Israel I have seen mortar between the stones in walls that were already old when Jesus walked the earth.

Every time you walk by a brick wall, you are seeing a memorial of the brick layer who built it. That memorial doesn't stand because of the bricks. It stands because of the mortar.

Mortar powder is only mortar powder. Water is just water. However, when the powder and the water are mixed together, they solidify and perpetually testify that the brick layer has been there.

The Mortar Of Your Memorial

When your prayers and your offerings are mixed together, they produce something greater than either of them can produce independently. They build a memorial that rises up into the presence of God, perpetually presenting the petitions of your heart to Him.

When Hannah made her vow to God, mixing it with her prayer, she literally memorialized her desire before God. Her request for a son took up perpetual residence in His sight. Because of that, the Lord remembered her, and His hand moved to open her womb. Hannah built a memorial!

It was the eleventh hour for the dear widow at Zarephath. Her prayers had gone up for months, but only one scant meal remained. When she gave it to the man of God, that act of giving turned her prayer into a memorial. Immediately the hand of God was moved into her empty barrel of meal and cruse of oil.

When the great man, Jephthah, faced pending disaster, without hesitation he built a memorial. He vowed to give God whatever He wanted from his possessions. He did so with the confidence that his prayer, mingled with his gift, would find its way into the presence of God. He knew it would swiftly move God's hand. Jephthah quickly formed his memorial prayer in the heat of battle, and just as quickly, the Lord joined him in the battle.

The Offering Must Be Valuable To You

Please notice the extreme value of each of these offerings. One woman gave her *firstborn son* – the son she had longed to have for many years. Another gave the *last bite of food* that stood between her and starvation. A judge gave God the choice of his possessions, *his only daughter.* A constant stream of offerings from a Roman centurion brought a *divinely commissioned apostle to his door.* All of these valuable gifts, along with fervent prayers, built memorials before God that caused His hand to move on their behalf.

Truth Continues Into The New Testament

With the introduction of Cornelius' memorial prayer, we see that this method of prayer was not limited to the Old Testament. In the tenth chapter of Acts we find the clearest explanation of all.

Possibly Cornelius did not understand exactly what he was doing. That is evidenced by the fact that the angel had to explain to him what he had done. Nevertheless, his love for God, coupled with his obedience to His Word, built a memorial that gave him the distinct honor of being *the first Gentile Christian.*

We Are Not Left To Stumble

Thank God that we have not been left to stumble upon this wonderful way of communicating our needs to God. This powerful method of prayer is clearly laid out for us from one end of Scripture to the other. We have seen case after case of desperate people who moved the hand of God to action. They were able to bring divine intervention to the point of their greatest needs with memorial prayer.

Please don't think you already know all there is to know about this subject. Our study of memorial prayer is far from complete. Much more information and confirmation must be revealed to you. Continue to read, for soon you will have the complete revelation and can start putting it to work in your own life.

6

Before She Asked, The Lord Knew

> . . . she of her *want* did cast in all that she had, even all her living.
>
> **Mark 12:44**

Most Christians are amazed when they learn exactly what Jesus taught about the poor widow of Mark 12. When teaching from that portion of Scripture, I usually ask the congregation where they think they would find Jesus if they were sent to look for Him in the temple.

People are never at a loss for an answer. Some say He would be found *where the prayers were being offered.* Others say He would surely be found *where the people were involved in praise and worship.* Some say He would surely be *where the scholars gathered to discuss the Scripture.*

Sitting In Front Of The Offering Plate

I wish you could stand with me in the pulpit and see the people's faces when I tell them they would probably not find Jesus in the places they suggested. Instead, He would be in the area *where people were giving the offering.* Yes, you read right. He actually seated Himself directly in front of the offering plate where He could watch the people as they gave their money.

Please notice what the Bible says. In this account, not only was Jesus watching *how much* the people gave, but He was especially interested in *how* they gave. He wanted to know what was going on *inside* them when they gave their offerings.

> . . . **Jesus sat over against the treasury, and** *beheld how the people cast* **money into the treasury: and many that were rich cast in much.**
>
> **And there came a certain poor widow, and she threw in two mites, which make a farthing.**
> **Mark 12:41,42**

If it had not been for Dr. Oral Roberts, I probably would never have noticed a most significant thing about this story. One night just prior to the "Praise the Lord" program at Trinity Broadcasting Network, Dr. Roberts opened his Bible and showed me something about the way the little widow gave her offering that I have never forgotten.

He pointed out to me that the *King James Version* of the Bible notes a difference between the way the rich people put their large sums of money into the treasury and the way the poor widow put her two mites into the treasury. In verse 41 the *King James Version* says the rich *cast* in their money. However, the next verse tells us that the widow *threw* in her money.

> **And there came a certain poor widow, and she**
> ***threw* in two mites, which make a farthing.**
> **Mark 12:42**

In those words, "she *threw* in two mites," the King James translators showed her desperation.

As Brother Roberts and I discussed that verse, suddenly a light came on, and I saw something that answered many of my questions.

All Offerings Are Not Equal

There was a vast difference between the offerings of the rich and the offering of the poor widow. Granted, the rich gave significantly larger sums of money, but what the widow gave was an infinitely greater offering. The large sums of money the rich cast in were of a different level of importance to their lives than the widow's offering was to her life. The Bible says they gave their large offerings out of their abundance. It was money left after they met their basic needs. It was *excess money* to them, or as I commonly refer to it, it was discretionary income.

When the widow gave, she gave money that was necessary for her survival. She gave money she needed to pay her bills, *for she was living on those two mites!*

Now, please don't let the philosophy of man or your own reasoning get in the way. The Word of God says the money she threw in was enough for her to live on.

> . . . she of her want did cast in all that she had, *even all her living.*
> **Mark 12:44**

Traditional Interpretations Had To Go

When Brother Roberts pointed out the last few words to me, it seemed unreasonable. Throughout my Christian life I had been taught that those two mites were an insignificant, little bit of money. The first thing that went through my mind was, "How could she live on just two, puny, little mites?"

Upon a closer examination of the weights and measures of that day, I found that two mites were equivalent to what was called "four pennies." Now, I know that doesn't sound like much money to us in this day. However, it sounds like much more when you realize that a Roman soldier earned about sixteen pennies a day.

With that information, everything started making more sense. What the widow actually threw in was twenty-five percent of a Roman soldier's daily pay. Why, if she was really careful, she could squeak out an existence on that amount. Of course, she would have to buy only the bare essentials; but let me emphasize, I have seen single mothers live on far less than half of what most people consider to be the bare essentials.

Unscriptural Traditions Hide The Truth

How much further the Church would be today if it weren't for the traditional teachings of men! As I said, I had been taught that the widow's two mites were so insignificant, they would not have done her any good if she had kept them. The Bible is surely correct when it says *our traditions make the Word of God of no effect* (Mark 7:13). Without the traditional teaching on that verse, I would have known her offering was very significant, for the Bible clearly says *she was living on it.*

> *. . . she . . . cast in . . . all her living.*
> **Mark 12:44**

Every bit of those two mites was money she desperately needed to meet her needs. It was precious money to her, for it actually represented all that stood between her family and starvation.

Giving To Receive

I am certain that the widow had heard all her life of God's desire to bless His children. She had often heard that her God, Jehovah, was a good God. She knew *He would give generously* to her if only she had the faith to *give generously to Him.*

As I have observed giving through my twenty-five-plus years in the ministry, I have often seen people reach into their pockets and place their loose change in the offering plate. Those folks never seem to blink an eye as they do nothing more than *tip* God. Most Christians can more easily trust God with their eternal souls than they can with their hard-earned money. Think of it! They trust Him with their *eternity,* but they are reluctant to trust Him with their *next meal.*

How different the poor widow's attitude was as she trusted God with the money she needed for her daily existence! There is no question that she was a woman who believed God, for she was at the temple. It is clear that she understood the relationship between giving to God and her release from poverty. Why else would she have been at the treasury?

Can't you just imagine what her thoughts might have been as she watched the rich casting vast sums of money into the treasury. They were giving amounts that would easily have met her every need and desire. No doubt the devil reasoned with her that God would not even notice her pitiful, little offering.

Quick Action Blocked Fear

In just another moment, the fear of insufficiency would have caused her to walk away, but she cast down those evil imaginations — ideas that would stop her from giving. Suddenly she realized that fear was about to overtake her, and just before it closed her hand on her four little pennies, she rose up and *violently threw them into the treasury!* With that desperate action, she ended the argument with the devil. Nothing could stop her from giving to her God, for the pennies had been launched, and they were headed straight for the offering plate.

Violent Action Captured Jesus' Attention

That widow's abrupt action is a perfect picture of exactly what the Bible says about those who get the victory.

> . . . the kingdom of heaven suffereth violence,
> and the violent take it by force.
> Matthew 11:12

With one violent move, she laid hold on the attention of God. Don't miss what happened next, for immediately Jesus looked up at her. Not only had she captured His full attention, but He audibly responded to her faith. He even cried out to His disciples bringing their attention to bear on her.

> And he called unto him his disciples, and
> saith unto them, Verily I say unto you, That *this
> poor widow* hath cast more in, than all they which
> have cast into the treasury.
> Mark 12:43

Notice that not one of the big gifts from the rich got a single response, but not so with the poor widow. Her gift made its impact. It did what she sent it to do. It drew the Lord's attention to her *want*.

The Greater Gift Is Not Always
The Biggest Gift

There is a great Bible truth I want to point out here. The world always looks at things differently from how the Lord does. In the world, people always take note of the amount a person gives. The *larger the gift,* the more attention it draws. The person who gives $1,000.00 always receives more recognition from the crowd than the one who gives only $10.00.

That is not the way God looks at giving. He always looks at things differently from the way we do.

> . . . man looketh on the outward appearance,
> but the Lord looketh on the heart.
> 1 Samuel 16:7

God Judges By How Much Is Left

When the Lord looks at a financial gift, surely He takes note of how much is given, but He goes beyond that because He also takes note of *how much the giver has left after He has given.* The person who gives $1,000.00 may have many thousands of dollars left after he gives. The person who gives $10.00 may have only $1.00 left. In God's eyes, that makes the $10.00 gift infinitely larger than the $1,000.00 gift.

Do not ever forget this principle. It will guide you in knowing how to get God's attention with a financial gift. *God always sees how much is left after giving!*

> . . . she. . . cast in *all that she had.* . . .
> **Mark 12:44**

She Wanted Something

Jesus said she was the biggest giver of the day. Remember, she was not one of those who casually cast in some insignificant amount from her excess. She had out-given all of them by *violently throwing in everything she had.* It was literally all of her living. However, not only had the Lord discerned the urgent manner in which she gave, but He realized she *wanted something* from Him.

We are never told exactly what she wanted. It could have been almost anything, for even when the needs of a poor widow are met, she still has many *unfulfilled wants.* While the details of her desire are not mentioned, we definitely know *she wanted something.*

Read every word of the account as carefully as you wish, but you will find that she did not audibly speak one word about wanting anything. However, as the handful of desperately thrown pennies fell into the offering container, *her Lord knew she wanted something from Him!*

> . . . she of her *want* did cast in all that she
> had, even all her living.
>
> **Mark 12:44**

That statement by our Lord lets us know that her two mites were a part of a memorial prayer!

I don't know how much theology the widow knew. I don't know how much she knew about the history-changing events that were about to be ushered in by Jesus. I do know she understood more about memorial prayer than the theologians of our day. *She knew how to get God's attention*, for as soon as her offering hit the plate, Jesus declared to His disciples *that she wanted something.*

The Case Is Proved

No Bible believer who has read this far can deny the existence of memorial prayer any longer. *Hannah* used it to move the hand of God to open her closed womb. The *widow at Zarephath* used it to draw the hand of God into her rapidly dwindling barrel of meal. *Jephthah* used memorial prayer to move the hand of God swiftly into the battle against the Ammonites. *Cornelius* used it to move God's hand to the rooftop to awaken Simon Peter. Then the *poor widow* of Mark 12 used memorial prayer to move God's hand to her want.

Be it a *centurion*, a *judge* in Israel, a *rich man's wife*, or a *poor widow*, God is ready to hear those who come to Him with memorial prayer.

No greater witness of memorial prayer is needed. However, there is still another great example in Scripture.

7

A Church Built A Memorial

*. . . no church communicated with me as
concerning *giving and receiving,* but ye only.*
Philippians 4:15

By now I hope you realize that you are not reading
the mere thoughts of a man, but you are reading of a
biblical principle of God. The truth of memorial prayer
may be quickly brushed aside by the *traditionalists.*
However, there is no denying that it is clearly taught in
the Bible. *Lay hold of this thought!* If it is taught in
God's Word, it becomes more than just an event in
Scripture. It becomes your right as a child of God.

A Church-Wide Memorial Prayer

I would like to take you even further into this
revelation. I would now like to bring you the witness of
several hundred, possibly even several thousand
Christians — people who successfully practiced *mingling
their prayers with their offerings* to receive from God. I
am speaking of the entire church congregation at
Philippi.

In the fourth chapter of Philippians, the Apostle Paul wrote words to this special church that have been misunderstood by most.

> . . . *no church* communicated with me as concerning *giving and receiving, but ye only.*
> Philippians 4:15

Once Again, Tradition Had Blocked Revelation

Until recently I did not understand the true significance of those words. I had always been taught that the Philippians were the only church who supported the Apostle Paul in his world outreach. Upon dropping the traditional explanation, I realized that was not what Paul was saying. That explanation of the Philippians being Paul's only supporting church does not agree with other scriptures. The Book of 2 Corinthians tells us that Paul's missionary work was *supported by many churches.*

> I robbed other churches [plural], taking wages of them, *to do you service.*
> 2 Corinthians 11:8

Paul, like Jesus, had a donor base that helped him go from city to city. His donors regularly sent him the financial support he needed. They consisted primarily of churches he had previously established. The above verse clearly tells us that the saints at Corinth had been recipients of Paul's ministry at the expense of several other churches. With that information in mind, it became necessary to find another reason for Paul's statement to the Philippians.

> . . . no church communicated with me as concerning giving and receiving, but ye only.
> **Philippians 4:15**

Memorial Prayer At Philippi

Please open your mind to the fact that the church at Philippi was engaged in *a very special type of giving agreement* with Paul. That is why he said the Philippians were *the only ones* who gave into his ministry in that special way. The arrangement they had entered into with the Apostle Paul was a *memorial prayer relationship.*

> Now ye Philippians know also, that in the beginning of the gospel, when I departed from Macedonia, no church communicated with me as *concerning giving and receiving* [giving with the expectation of receiving], but ye only.
> **Philippians 4:15**

Their giving relationship with Paul was unique. It was different from the giving of any other church, *for they gave expecting to receive something specific from God.* Paul's letter to them gives us a hint as to what it was they wanted, for he said:

> . . . my God *shall supply all your need* according to his riches in glory by Christ Jesus.
> **Philippians 4:19**

There it is. The context shows they wanted their needs supplied at a higher standard, so they must have been praying for *a better lifestyle*. Paul's promise to them shows that better lifestyle would be granted in the same *quality* as the standard enjoyed by God.

The Promise Might Not Be Yours

Before we go any further, let me say that Christians have also misunderstood Philippians 4:19. They have erroneously interpreted it to mean that God will automatically meet every Christian's need out of His riches in glory. However, after careful study, any honest Bible student will have to admit that it teaches no such thing!

In the first place, the verse does not say God would supply the recipients' needs *out of* His riches in glory, but *according to* His riches in glory. The word *according* means that something is to be of the same quality. The verse is actually saying that God would begin to meet the needs of the Philippians in a quality that would be comparable to the quality of His riches in glory.

In the second place, it is not a promise to all Christians, as many have supposed it to be. Paul directed it to a specific group of believers. The context clearly teaches that *the Philippian saints were the only church who gave into Paul's ministry with a specific request attached to their gift.* No other church gave in that way. They, and they alone communicated (gave) to Paul concerning giving *and* receiving.

God's Answer Had Come

Now, why would the Apostle make such a promise to them? It is plain that it was God's answer to their memorial prayer. The context indicates that the request they were making was for the quality of their lives to be improved, and God was now granting that request. Paul promised that from then on God would be supplying them with a higher standard of living.

God Does Not Meet The Needs Of Every Saint

One thing I know for certain is that Philippians 4:19 *is not* a promise from God to meet the needs of everyone in the body of Christ. Scripture clearly teaches that under certain circumstances, God will not meet the needs of some Christians.

> . . . if any would not work, neither should he eat.
>
> 2 Thessalonians 3:10

> . . . seek ye first the kingdom of God, and his righteousness; and all these things shall be added unto you.
>
> Matthew 6:33

I have heard well-meaning people say the Bible promises that not one of God's children will ever have to *beg for bread.* They quote the following verse to prove their point:

> I have been young, and now am old; yet have I not seen the righteous forsaken, nor his seed begging bread.
>
> **Psalm 37:25**

Very seldom do I hear that verse used correctly. Most Christians assume that the seed spoken of is the seed of God. Nothing in the context even hints that the words *his seed* refer to "God's seed." King David did not say he never saw God's children begging bread. He said that through his entire life, he never saw the children of a truly righteous man begging for bread.

> . . . yet have I not seen the righteous forsaken, nor his seed [the seed of the righteous] begging bread.
>
> **Psalm 37:25**

It is common knowledge that there are saints who beg daily. There is even Scripture that backs it up.

> . . . there was a certain *beggar* named Lazarus, which was laid at his gate, full of sores,
>
> And *desiring to be fed* with the crumbs which fell from the rich man's table: moreover the dogs came and licked his sores.
>
> And it came to pass, that *the beggar died*, and was carried by the angels into Abraham's bosom: the rich man also died, and was buried.
>
> **Luke 16:20-22**

Surely Lazarus was one of God's children, for at his death the angels carried him to the bosom of Father

Abraham. Yet the Word of God says he was begging bread. Not only that, but the Word calls him a beggar. By no stretch of the imagination can it be said that his needs were being supplied according to God's riches in glory.

When he spoke of never seeing the righteous man's children begging bread, David was speaking of the same truth Solomon wrote about in the Book of Proverbs.

> **A good man leaveth an inheritance to his children's children. . . .**
> **Proverbs 13:22**

That verse clearly teaches that the good man will leave an inheritance to his children and grandchildren, thereby ensuring that they (his seed) will never have to beg bread.

With those proof texts I hope the assumption that God will supply every Christian's need according to His riches in glory is put to rest. Philippians 4:19 is a promise the Apostle Paul relayed to the Philippians. It was God's answer to the memorial prayer request they had made by giving into his ministry.

It Still Works Today

A few months ago one of our partners shared that his standard of living began to improve after he started giving regularly to our ministry. He said he had found our ministry to be good ground for planting his seed and that he had been praying for his lifestyle to improve. At that time I did not fully understand the meaning of Philippians 4:15-19. Now I know that he, like the Philippians, was mixing his prayers with his gifts to build a memorial prayer for a better lifestyle. Or it might be said, as Paul said to the Philippians, he had been communicating with our ministry concerning giving and receiving.

A Better Lifestyle Is Not Wrong

Let me quickly say that there is nothing wrong with a better lifestyle. God doesn't receive any special glory when His children ride around in unsafe vehicles. His goodness is not made known to the world by Christians living in bad neighborhoods. Exposing our children to the cocaine dealers and the ghetto environment is not a badge of righteousness. God receives no glory over Christians sleeping in homes with poor heating systems. He receives no honor because Christians cannot afford to send their children to college. He doesn't especially rejoice over the family who can never afford to give to world missions. What glory does God receive when His children watch a Christian telethon and are not able to give?

Child of God, wake up! A better lifestyle is within the will of God for you! The Word of God clearly says it is.

> . . . no *good thing* will he withhold from them that walk uprightly.
>
> Psalm 84:11

Let the Lord be magnified, which hath pleasure in the prosperity of his servant.

Psalm 35:27

Beloved, I wish above all things that thou mayest prosper and be in health, even as thy soul prospereth.

3 John 2

Piercing Traditional Darkness

The tradition of poverty in the Church has put many of God's children into the tightest financial conditions imaginable. Then to add insult to injury, many misguided Church leaders cause their people to reject the truth of God's abundant supply. If it were not for the Christians who dare to boldly press into God's Word, the world would never be won.

Thank God for the scriptural account, for by it we can see so many of His truths displayed in the lives of others. The Philippian request for a better lifestyle boldly speaks that which most Christians only wish for but do not dare to ask. They were special saints, for they built a memorial prayer that moved the hand of God. The scriptural record shines through the darkness of tradition telling us of people who dared to ask for a better lifestyle, and they got it!

. . . my God shall supply all your need *according to his riches in glory by Christ Jesus.*

Philippians 4:19

Remember, you must *ask* if you want to receive. You must *knock* if you want new doors to open. You must *seek* before you will find.

> **Ask, and it shall be given you; seek, and ye shall find; knock, and it shall be opened unto you.**
> **Matthew 7:7**

If you think back over the past chapters, you will see that I have shown you memorial prayer from one end of the Scripture to the other. In the following chapters I will begin to deal specifically with *how you can build a memorial that will move the hand of God on behalf of your greatest need.*

8

The Proper Finances Of
The Memorial Prayer

> . . . this also that she hath done shall be spoken of for a memorial of her.
>
> **Mark 14:9**

Up to this point of our study, we have not yet dealt with the step-by-step procedure that must be taken to build a memorial prayer. I have diligently searched the Scripture for the exact instructions. For a very long time the answer seemed to elude me. Then one day God showed me exactly how it is done.

Building a memorial has two specific parts: praying and giving. In this chapter I will show you from the Bible how to properly perform the financial portion of your memorial.

Many Different Types Of Memorials Exist

A study on the subject will quickly show you that there are many different types of memorials mentioned in Scripture. There are memorial names, memorial offerings, memorial ceremonies, memorial structures, memorial clothing, and even memorial adornments. God showed me that while the Bible speaks of many different types of memorials, they are all pretty much the same in their structure.

Everyone knows there is a difference between a community house and a church house. However, the basic structural components of both buildings are the same. The beams, walls, and foundations are constructed by the same principles of engineering.

With that truth in mind, let's begin to study the actions of a very pious woman who, through her giving, built an eternal memorial. Please keep in mind that while this illustration does not specifically pertain to building a memorial prayer, it does show how to properly give to establish a memorial.

The Woman With The Alabaster Box

The account we will now study is found in the fourteenth chapter of Mark. In this portion of Scripture, a woman brought a special gift to Jesus.

> . . . there came a woman having an alabaster box of ointment of spikenard very precious; and she brake the box, and poured it on his head.
> Mark 14:3

Oil of spikenard was a valuable perfumed oil. It was in great demand by the very rich of her day. According to the context, that box of perfume had a value of more than *three hundred pence.*

> **For it might have been sold for more than three hundred pence. . . .**
>
> Mark 14:5

Today's Value Must Be Established

Establishing the dollar value of her ointment according to today's standards is rather difficult due to the severe inflation the world economic system has suffered over the last 2,000 years. However, it is known that during the time of Christ, three hundred pence were equal to the annual wages of the average working person. It could easily have been worth $18,000 to $24,000 compared to the wages of the average American.

That amount must be left subject to adjustment since oil of spikenard was one of the ultimate luxuries in the time of Christ. It would probably be worth somewhat less today as modern technology has brought about luxuries of a much greater value such as cars, airplanes, and yachts. Using the best perfumes of our day as a price comparison, let's say it would be worth several thousand dollars. No matter how you figure it, that perfume was a very expensive gift to say the least.

Giving Often Brings Man's Disapproval

Notice that when the woman gave the expensive gift, some of the believers watching her did not approve of her actions.

> And there were some that *had indignation*
> within themselves. . . .
>
> **Mark 14:4**

That reaction is characteristic with some who hear about memorial prayer. Many of them are immediately indignant. Some would become upset if their pastor were to even intimate that a person's giving has anything to do with God's response to his prayers.

Notice that those who were filled with indignation were not against the woman giving. They simply wanted her to give in such a way that they would be able to decide how her money would be spent. They immediately cried out that she was not making the best use of her ointment.

That same account in the Book of John says that the main spokesman was none other than Judas. He protested, saying she should have sold the oil and used the money for the poor, not because he had some great love for the poor, but because he wanted to steal the money. Hear the Apostle John's version:

**Then saith one of his disciples, Judas
Iscariot, Simon's son, which should betray him,**

**Why was not this ointment sold for three
hundred pence, and given to the poor?**

**This he said, not that he cared for the poor;
but because he was a thief, and had the bag, and
bare [had control of] what was put therein.**
John 12:4-6

How typical that is of the mentality of many in the
church of our day. Many times those who are on the
church board want, more than anything else, to dictate
what is to be done with the money people give. Too
often those same so-called pillars are among the lowest
givers in the church.

I have been called to the pastorate of three different
churches in my lifetime. In each case I found board
members who did not tithe. One of the first things I
always did as pastor was to ask those non-tithers to
either start giving tithes and offerings or give up their
positions on the board. That stand did not always make
me popular, but it always did put the control of church
finances into the hands of proper givers.

Notice how those who were filled with indignation
tried to make the woman feel bad. They pointed out
that her gift had been unwisely spent and that she
should have given it to the poor. (Isn't it strange how
many people who cry out on behalf of the poor hardly
ever give anything to them?)

Jesus Approved

No sooner had they begun to voice their disapproval than our Lord spoke the words that put the woman at ease.

And Jesus said, *let her alone; why trouble ye her?* **she hath** *wrought a good work on me.*
Mark 14:6

How comforting those words have been to my wife and me during the times when the gainsayers have risen up against us to criticize our giving. Sometimes that criticism has come from our closest loved ones and relatives. At those times we must simply rest in the wonderful words of Jesus, "Let them alone. Why are you troubling them? They are doing a *good work for me.*"

Child of God, as you start to build your first memorial, please let the words of Jesus speak comfort to your spirit. The thing you are about to do *is a good thing.*

Giving To God Is The Ultimate Giving

Jesus went on to tell them to take every opportunity they could to be in relationship with Him. They could give money to the poor anytime they wanted, for the poor would always be around. He would not be with them forever.

> . . . ye have the poor with you always, and
> whensoever ye will ye may do them good: but me ye
> have not always.
>
> Mark 14:7

I want you to take note. There are special times when each one of us must come away from all the things we could be doing and make contact with Jesus. The woman with the alabaster box could minister to the poor any day she wished, but that particular day was her special chance to minister to Jesus.

My mind goes back to the many memorial prayer requests my wife and I have made. Each time there were literally hundreds of other things we could have done with our money. Still we deemed it more important to press into our Lord's presence and bring His special attention to focus on a specific need. As we would mingle our money with our prayers, it was always comforting to know He approved of what we were doing. We could just imagine Him saying, "Just leave John and Patricia alone. They are doing a good work on me."

You Must Give All That You Can

There is another important aspect to the financial portion of building a memorial prayer. Jesus made it plain that the woman's gift was made up of more than just some loose change in her pocket. It was a substantial gift. It was actually all she could possibly give at that time.

She hath done *what she could.* . . .
Mark 14:8

Those words do not mean she did only that which was permitted. They mean she had done *all she was able to do.*

You will never build a memorial prayer with a tip. You must remember that the financial gift you give to God must be an expression of the urgency of your request and the sincerity of your heart. The memorial prayer offering should be a symbol of your laying a piece of your life before the altar of God.

A good rule of thumb in deciding how much you should give to build your memorial prayer is: If your offering *doesn't move you, it won't move God.*

A Proper Gift Built An Eternal Memorial Of Her Life

In the next verse we see exactly what the alabaster box of ointment meant to God. Jesus said that the dear woman had made a perpetual memorial of her life *through her giving.*

Verily I say unto you, Wheresoever this gospel shall be preached throughout the whole world, this also that she hath done shall be spoken of for a *memorial of her.*

Mark 14:9

Those were true words spoken by our Savior, for ever since that day people have known the woman with the alabaster box. Every generation since has heard her story. Notice that she did not *write a book* or *build a church*. She did not *lead any great crusades*. Nevertheless, all the Church knows her. Her properly funded memorial has stood throughout all generations.

Her gift was of such quality that it built a memorial to her forever. That kind of giving will also build a memorial prayer for you.

9

The Prayer Of The Memorial

> . . . ye may prove [experience] what is that
> good, and acceptable, and perfect, will of God.
> **Romans 12:2**

While we can easily see how the woman in Mark 14 established a memorial by giving properly, we must look more deeply to find out how to make the prayer request of the memorial. There is a truth we must always keep in mind when we form the words of our prayers. We must pray only for those things that are in agreement with the will of God.

> . . . this is the confidence that we have in him,
> that, *if we ask any thing according to his will,* he
> heareth us.
> **1 John 5:14**

How To Know What To Pray

God clearly states that He will hear only those prayers that are in accordance with His will. You may wonder how in the world we can know the will of God. *First,* we must be students of the Bible, for without studying the Word of God, we will never know His will.

> **Study to shew thyself approved unto God, a workman** *that needeth not to be ashamed,* **rightly dividing the word of truth.**
> **2 Timothy 2:15**

The Renewed Mind Knows His Will

The study of God's Word will *renew your mind,* causing you to know the perfect will of God.

> **. . . be not conformed to this world: but be ye transformed** *by the renewing of your mind,* **that ye may prove [experience] what is** *that good, and acceptable, and perfect, will of God.*
> **Romans 12:2**

The Willingness To Change

Next, you must be soft and pliable to God's will for your life. You must be ready to replace your thoughts and desires with the thoughts and desires of God. That may sound difficult at first, but it is actually easy when you submit to the process God has prescribed for bringing it to pass.

Delight thyself also in the Lord; and *he shall give thee the desires of thine heart.*

Commit thy way unto the Lord; trust also in him; and he shall bring it to pass.
Psalm 37:4,5

That portion of Scripture always brings much peace to those who read it in its proper context. In verse four, the first word was translated by the King James writers as *delight*. The original Hebrew word used there literally means "to be soft and pliable." In other words, "Be soft and pliable in the hand of God, and He will give you the desires of your heart."

If that were all God had to say on the matter, we would have to conclude that He would give us whatever we wanted as long as we were soft and pliable in His hands. However, if that were the meaning, we would all soon be in big trouble. Most of our own desires are not God's desires for us. Bear with me and I will show you that is not what God is saying.

He will not give you whatever you desire if you just delight yourself in Him. God is saying He will cause our desires to be taken out of our hearts and His own desires to be put into our hearts. As we become *soft and pliable* in His hand, the things we desire will become the same things He desires.

Now, look at verse five again, for you cannot fully understand verse four without understanding verse five.

119

Commit thy way unto the Lord; trust also in him; and he shall bring it to pass.
Psalm 37:5

The *King James Version* begins with the word *commit.* The exact meaning of that word is "to roll" or "to place." Let us now paraphrase the verse using that meaning.

Roll the responsibility of deciding the way you must go onto the Lord [let Him plan your way]; trust in Him, and He will bring *it* to pass.

Notice that little word *it.* What is the *it* God promises to bring to pass for those who roll the responsibility of deciding their way on Him? The *it* is the desire of your heart mentioned in verse four. Not only will God put certain desires in your heart, but if you commit your way to Him, He will bring those desires to pass.

Now, let's look at both verses together again with this new understanding.

Be soft and pliable in the hand of God, and He will replace your old desires with His own new desires.

Roll the responsibility of deciding the way you must go onto the Lord. Trust in Him, and He will bring to pass those new, God-given desires that you allowed Him to put into your heart.

Whenever you build a memorial prayer, *you must be sure that what you are asking for is God's will in the matter.* Remember, the Apostle John said if we ask *according to God's will*, He hears us.

> . . . this is the confidence that we have in him, that, if we ask any thing according to his will, *he heareth us.*
>
> **1 John 5:14**

God hears the prayers that are according to His Word. With that thought in mind, read from the Book of Job.

> Thou shalt *make thy prayer* unto him, and *he shall hear thee*, and thou shalt *pay thy vows.*
>
> Thou shalt also *decree a thing, and it shall be established unto thee.* . . .
>
> **Job 22:27,28**

Isn't it amazing how the memorial prayer is popping up everywhere since you began this study? There it is in Job. *Make your prayer* (the prayer part), *pay your vow* (the money part), and *it shall be established unto you* (the answer is assured).

Now, notice that it also says God will hear. That means the prayer must be one God can agree with. I say that because Scripture says God hears only if we pray according to His will.

> . . . this is the confidence that we have in him, that, *if we ask any thing according to his will, he heareth us.*
>
> **1 John 5:14**

Directing God's hand is possible only to those who know His will. Do not let that thought throw you. His will is discernible. It is freely given to us in His Word. Anytime you pray—especially if you are building a memorial prayer—always pray what the Word says.

If you are praying for a lost man, always pray for his salvation, because God says He is not willing that any should perish.

> **The Lord is . . . not willing that any should perish, but that all should come to repentance.**
> **2 Peter 3:9**

If you are praying for finances, always boldly pray for the supply you need, for He clearly states that He wants you to prosper.

> **Beloved, I wish above all things that thou mayest prosper and be in health, even as thy soul prospereth.**
> **3 John 2**

If you pray for brothers or sisters in Christ, pray only those things that will uplift them and bring them into God's best for their lives.

> **. . . whatsoever things are true, whatsoever things are honest, whatsoever things are just, whatsoever things are pure, whatsoever things are lovely, whatsoever things are of good report; if there be any virtue, and if there be any praise, think on these things.**
> **Philippians 4:8**

Always pray what the Word of God says, and God will always hear you. *When you pray the Word, you are praying according to His will.*

Remember these two steps when you build your memorial prayer:
1. You must give *a proper offering.*
2. You must pray *an acceptable prayer.*

Now, place your proper offering and your acceptable prayer together. Let God know they are not individual items, but they are mixed together to form a memorial.

Be sure the ministry to which you choose to give your offering understands the truth of memorial giving. Include a brief word about your prayer request, and ask that ministry to stand in faith with you, believing that your memorial prayer will quickly move the hand of God to your point of need.

Every day our ministry holds up hundreds of memorial prayers in agreement before God. Our office staff, as well as my wife and I, pray over each one we receive for at least one month. It is important that the ministry you choose gives this same kind of care to your memorial prayer.

10

Memorials Work Daily In My Life

> ... they overcame him by ... the word of their testimony. ...
>
> **Revelation 12:11**

So much of Christianity is based on theory. While they may be interesting, theories do not release the power of God.

For many years the Church accepted theories. However, people who serve God today want something that works. They are turned off by a Christianity that is based on mere theory.

Theological discussions about peace will not satisfy the troubled. Stories of healing that took place twenty years ago will not meet the needs of those who are sick today. Songs about power will not give the victory to the weak. The Word of God should be verified by more than just a chapter and verse. Yes, it is to be verified by chapter and verse, but it should also be accompanied by signs and wonders.

People today are not going to get saved just because the Bible says Jesus saves. They will be drawn to God when they see the transformed lives of those who are already saved and overcoming sin. Cripples no longer find their way to miracle rallies because the Bible tells them they are healed with His stripes. They come because of the signs and wonders of other cripples walking, blind eyes being opened, and the deaf hearing.

Today tangible proof must accompany the doctrines of healing, salvation, and deliverance. That which is being taught must be manifested. By that same rule of human nature, most people will try memorial prayer only if they see its effectiveness manifested. To put it plainly, if what I teach *doesn't work,* it really *isn't worth knowing.*

In this chapter I will share some memorial prayers my wife and I have made. These prayers moved the hand of God swiftly and directly to the point of our need. Pat and I know they worked, and many others witnessed that they worked in our lives.

Proper Bookings For A Traveling Ministry

Several years ago my wife and I gave up the pastorate of our church in Joplin, Missouri. We left behind the security of a regular salary and everything we had ever worked for. When we departed, we had only one speaking engagement booked.

You must realize that our move was not the adventure of a couple of young kids. We had already reached mid-life. We knew that if the new ministry didn't work, we would suffer for our mistake throughout our senior years.

Two months before we left Joplin, we made a significant memorial prayer request. That memorial is still functioning as I write this chapter several years later.

The equity in our home represented the greater portion of our assets at that time. We had put $45,000 down on the house. No one would have argued with the fact that it would have been good business to sell it and carefully guard the profit from the sale.

Instead of holding on to our equity, we decided to use it as the financial portion of our memorial. We knew that our greatest need was not to have the $45,000 in the bank. Our greatest need was to have speaking engagements in good churches every week. If we kept the $45,000, how far could it go? Why, even if we were careful, it would last only a short time. However, if we could receive plenty of good bookings, they would provide more than enough income for many years to come.

We were facing the same dilemma you face every time the offering plate is passed your way. Should you trust the money, or should you trust God? We decided that without speaking engagements, we would be destined to face the same disappointments that many traveling ministries face — sporadic bookings which cause constant insufficiency. That arrangement would quickly bring our work to a close, for a ministry that teaches God's abundance cannot operate in shortage.

We Trusted God Instead Of The Money

We gave the $45,000 equity to the church we were leaving and made our request for bookings known to God. We prayed, "God, we must have quality bookings. There must be speaking engagements every Sunday and Wednesday and as many days in between as possible." Well, only a few days passed before God began to move above and beyond anything we had imagined.

We arrived at my one and only speaking engagement at the annual convention of a large ministry. I spoke three times that week and received a modest honorarium. On the last night of the meeting, I went to the closing banquet without a single booking ahead of me. I must admit, it was not the most confident evening of my life. Memories of the words several people had spoken to me filled my head. Most of those who knew my plans had said I was a fool to leave the security of my pulpit in Joplin. They did not believe I would have enough bookings to make ends meet. Besides that, the devil had told me I would soon see that memorial prayers did not really work.

The only positive note I heard that night was from my dear wife, Pat. She reminded me several times of the faithfulness of our God. She said our prayer had been memorialized, and it was lingering in God's presence at that very moment.

At the close of that evening's activities, as we walked from the banquet hall, the pastor of a church in the area approached me. Almost apologetically he told me his church was a small one. He knew I would probably not come, but he had felt the leading of the Lord to ask me to minister to his congregation. He wondered if I would consider coming to his church sometime. When I said I would be glad to, he asked me when I thought that might be. Since the next day was Sunday, I asked, "How about in the morning?"

At first he did not believe I was serious, but I quickly assured him that I was. With that appointment, I had a booking for my first Sunday out of Joplin.

Later that night the evangelist in charge of the convention called my room and invited me to go with him to South Africa for 21 days. We would leave the following Friday. He also included my wife and son in the invitation. As I looked at my calendar, I was happily surprised to see I had bookings for an entire month.

God was still at work on our memorial, for when I reached South Africa I was invited to stay and preach an extra week. Upon leaving that country, one of the local pastors invited me back and promised he would have places for me to preach every night and every Sunday morning for a month.

To make a long story short, in the first six months of our new ministry, we never missed a Sunday or Wednesday night of speaking, and we spoke many other nights in between. Not only that, but our bookings never dropped below six months in advance.

As I now write, our calendar is solidly booked for over one year in advance. When I say *solidly booked,* I mean almost every day of every month. At the time of this writing, I am home only an average of five days per month. It has truly happened to us as it happened to Cornelius. Our gifts and prayers are held in continual remembrance before God. The memorial of $45,000 we made is working better than we could have asked or thought. That is exactly what the Bible says about God's willingness to bless us.

> . . . [He] is able to do exceeding abundantly above all that we ask or think. . . .
> Ephesians 3:20

Paying Off An Office Building

Not too long ago our ministry purchased a new office building. We had outgrown the space we were using in our house. Then in less than six months, we also outgrew a rented facility.

The new building is beautiful, spacious, comfortable, and conveniently located near our home. When we moved in, it was much larger than we needed. In order to purchase the building, we took out a $225,000 loan.

I had planned to rent out the part we could not use to help pay off the note.

Just before we moved in, a precious minister friend of ours told us she was moving her ministry to the Fort Worth area. She related that she was under tremendous financial pressure at the time. She said her office furniture was already in transit to our city and asked if we knew of any economical office space that was available.

Pat and I immediately saw that her move was a tremendous opportunity for us. We would give her the office space she needed free of any cost. We told her we would charge only for utilities.

Now, you may ask, "Why would you do that? How could you call that an opportunity? You needed the rent to help make the new mortgage payment."

Child of God, open your spiritual ears! The rent from the office space could only help make *the monthly payment.* Our real desire was to *rapidly pay off the entire mortgage.* We needed to build a memorial prayer for an *early payoff of the $225,000 loan.* The need for a memorial was much more important than a few hundred dollars a month would be.

Now, don't misunderstand. The rent money would have alleviated pressure from our budget. It would have given us much needed surplus funds, for we still needed to purchase furniture and equipment to effectively utilize the new building.

Thank God we had the wisdom to move her into the office rent free, for the balance on our mortgage is now zero. It is paid in full. Even if we had charged our friend $1,000 per month in rent, it would only have helped us make our monthly mortgage payment. By making the office space into a memorial, we moved the hand of God to pay off the entire balance in a fraction of the time.

As I mentioned before, it was fully my intention to have our friend pay a portion of the utility bills. Each month when I began to tell her the amount she owed, the Spirit of God restrained me. Then God showed me why.

I had begun to realize that in time we would need even more office space than our new building would provide. When that time came, we would have to move to another location. I did not believe God wanted us to ever move again. However, we would be land-locked if anyone should ever build on the lot next to us. That would make future expansion impossible.

As I prayed about it, God showed me that if we bought the lot next door, we could later build an adequate addition to our present building. We didn't need the space right away, but if we didn't go ahead and buy the lot, there was no guarantee it would be available later.

At the Lord's prompting, I approached the owner about selling the lot. How exact the Holy Spirit is, for it was the perfect time. The owner offered to sell the lot for just about half the price he had quoted just a few months earlier. Needless to say, we bought it. We did not have all cash, but with a good down payment and a small mortgage of $20,000, we were well on the way to making it ours.

Immediately I realized that we needed an offering to make a memorial prayer for the rapid payoff of the lot. I knew just the thing to do. We would give our friend her utilities free. I hope you can see the powerful advantage of that arrangement. Through my monthly hesitation to ask for her utility payment, she had paid none for eight months. As I then mingled that amount of money with my request to have our new lot rapidly paid off, we built the memorial prayer.

As I write this page, we have fully paid off the lot years ahead of time. Once again our memorial prayer worked, and it worked faster than we thought possible.

We Placed A Retirement Plan With A Better Insurer

Pat and I recently made another memorial prayer. It has not yet borne fruit, but as you will see, there is still time before we will need it.

When a responsible person reaches his fifties, his mind usually turns to thoughts of financial security for the time when he will no longer work. Pat and I have no plans or any desire for retirement, but we do know a time is coming when we will at least want to slow down. When that happens there is a definite possibility that our earning potential will decrease.

We have checked into various retirement plans. One that caught our attention was a one-payment life insurance policy. With that form of insurance, you pay a single payment to a reputable insurance company, and it insures your life until you are sixty-five years old. Then it pays you a large sum of money.

We looked at several of those plans and found one that would give us enough income at age sixty-five for us to continue to minister without having to work quite as hard as we do now. Then when we saw the amount we would have to pay, it astounded us. The premium would be $104,000 cash. Wow! That's a lot of money! But that amount is not the most important thing. What is important is that retirement age is fast approaching.

With some serious pencil work, we realized that if we liquidated some of our assets, we could obtain that amount of money. However, when we looked at the dollars that would be made available to us at age sixty-five, we realized it might not be all that much — especially after we figured in several years of inflation.

Suddenly it came to us! If we invested the $104,000 in a memorial offering for our retirement, we just knew our God would bring us something better than the insurance company could. With that idea in mind, we gave the $104,000 to the Trinity Broadcasting Network. It was the largest single gift we had ever given to any one ministry.

I hope that example demonstrates to you that we not only teach the Word of God, but we also practice those principles we teach. Granted, at this writing the memorial prayer has not yet brought forth fruit, but we both rest easier knowing our retirement years are in the hands of God instead of the hands of an insurance company.

Please don't misunderstand. I am not against insurance. I am not against retirement plans. I am simply depending on God to lead me to something better than the plan I had. I believe God will soon enable us to purchase a retirement plan that will pay us much more per month than we need. I just know that after all our years of liberally giving to God, we will not be happy in our retirement if we do not have a surplus from which we can continue to give, even up to the day of His return.

Don't Be Scared Off

Before I scare someone away with the $45,000 and $104,000 memorials, let me assure you that we have made memorial prayers with much more modest sums. Even though the dollar amount of many of them was much less, please realize they represented just as much to us as the larger gifts did.

Let me emphasize again that there is not a set dollar amount that will move the hand of God in your memorial prayer. It is what that amount represents to you as the giver. The gifts Pat and I give today are no larger to God than the gifts we gave when we had almost nothing. Remember, it is the world that judges your offering by how much you have given. God always judges by how much is left *after you have given.* That truth is evident from Jesus' statement about the widow who threw in her two mites.

> . . . this poor widow hath cast more in, than all they which have cast into the treasury:
>
> For . . . she of her want did cast in all that she had, even all her living.
>
> **Mark 12:43,44**

Memorials Reach Beyond Financial Needs

Several years ago my second daughter experienced a tragic divorce. It seemed as if her life would never get straightened out. She and her three precious daughters had to move into the house with us, and she became dependent on us for a portion of her daily needs.

Not only did she have the regular needs that go with raising three children, but she also needed an education. As she went to school, the pressure from her situation became more and more pronounced. Even with all we were doing to help, she and her children were suffering a terrible void. We tried to be all we could be to her, but it wasn't enough. She needed a good helpmate. Even more, her children desperately needed a loving father.

One day as we ministered in Mexico, my wife said, "John, what our daughter needs is a good husband. He must be someone who will love her and help her and also love our precious grandchildren as if they were his own. Let's make a memorial prayer before God for the right man to come into her life — a special man who can make the whole family happy."

I asked how much she thought we should give, and she looked in the checkbook. After calculating the balance, she said we had a little over $300 left in our account. With that precious $300, we decided to make our memorial.

As we kneeled at the bed in our little Mexican hotel room, we carefully worded our prayer. We were very specific. We rehearsed all the good qualities and characteristics we expected our new son-in-law to have. Then we took the money and said, "We establish this memorial before you, God, and we trust your Word that it will be continually before you until you send the right man to our precious daughter."

Well, I have seldom seen God work faster. Before the month was over, a fine man came into our daughter's life. He was everything we had ever asked for and more. As I write this, my daughter is now married to him. He is a good husband, father, and son-in-law. Since they have been married, they have both come to work for our ministry. In a day when many second marriages are worse than the first, his appearance in our lives can be explained in only one way. The hand of God moved and brought Charles Flowers to our daughter, her children, and to our ministry.

God Reached Across
The North American Continent

I also have a son who works with us in the ministry. There was a period of time when he lived in California. While he was there, my wife had a horrible vision. In it she saw him being murdered. She was so shaken by the vision that we knew it was more than just a trick of the imagination. It was a warning from God.

Pat immediately called our son. From the conversation, she discerned that things were not well with him. She warned him of the pending danger and told him that if he did not change his lifestyle, irreparable damage would be done. He politely thanked her, but he paid no mind to what she had said.

When she hung up the phone, Pat said, "John, we must make a memorial prayer. If we don't, I feel the vision I saw will come to pass." I agreed with her.

We checked our finances, and by scraping, we came up with $500 which we gave to the Lord along with our request. "God, spare our son's life."

A few months passed without any word from him. Then suddenly our son called. He was terribly frightened because, true to the vision, his life was being threatened. Nothing can be gained by giving all the details, but let me say that God moved swiftly. Before that day was over he was in our home, hundreds of miles from those who would have harmed him. God brought him safely to his father's house, and today he is in full time ministry with us.

Thank God, we knew how to move the hand of God against the hand of the devil. Our son was not slain on the altar of this world, but he now serves at the altar of God.

An Old Feud Was Settled

Here is another illustration of a memorial that Pat and I built. Because of the delicacy of the subject, I will not be able to give many details, but I am sure this will bless you.

For several years, my wife had a less-than-smooth relationship with a certain family member. I am not saying they fought all the time, but for one reason or another, there was always friction between them.

One day we heard that relative was coming to visit us for a long stay. At first my wife became tense, but then she quickly said, "I am going to move the hand of God into this situation. We are going to be the best of friends."

With that she made out a check for $250 and prayed, "Lord, I am making a memorial prayer before you this day. This relative and I are going to become friends — good friends! We will flow together. The devil will not cause friction between us any longer!"

Thank God! There has never again been a cross word between them! That visit was the best ever, and now they can hardly wait to speak and visit with each other.

Our Abducted Grandchildren Immediately Released

The quickest response to memorial prayer we ever experienced took place in 1989. We were ministering through the central United States when we received the most distressing news we have ever heard.

It was early Saturday morning when our daughter-in-law, Kim, finally tracked us down in Dayton, Ohio. We were preparing to leave for the closing session of a School of Biblical Economics when I answered the phone. I knew something was wrong, for her voice was full of tears as I heard her say, "The children have been taken. They were visiting in another city, and they have been taken." A man had abducted them and told Kim she would never see them again.

I immediately began to rebuke the fear that tried to grip me. As I listened further, she said the police had gone to the man's house. They found he had moved and left no forwarding address. When they checked his place of employment, they found he had quit his job with no word of where he was going.

Because it was then nearly time to start the meeting, we prayed with Kim, comforting her as much as we could. We then left for the church. On the way, my wife said, "John, we must immediately make a memorial prayer to get Jesse and Jenny home safely."

When I heard those words, I had an immediate witness in my heart. I said, "That's what I'm teaching about this morning. We can do it during the lesson as an illustration."

Pat got out the checkbook, and with a few calculations came up with our best possible gift on such short notice, $500. I remember mentioning how different that same event would have been just a few years earlier. We would probably have canceled the meeting and dashed across the country to see about our family. That was before we had learned how to move the hand of God to our point of need.

At church I taught the people much of what I have taught you in this book. Then at the end, I told them of our bad news about our grandchildren. My wife came forward, and we demonstrated how to make a memorial prayer. We spoke plainly and clearly to the Lord that we knew it was not right for someone to take our grandchildren, and we knew He (God) was concerned. We told Him we had brought our best gift to Him. It represented our lives, for we had worked many long, hard hours to accumulate it. We further said we wanted Him to comfort and protect our grandchildren and to comfort our daughter-in-law. We asked that our grandchildren be returned to their mother safely at once.

After praying we put the money in an envelope with our request clearly written on the back. We placed it in the offering to the church where we were speaking and believed our request became a memorial in the presence of God.

The meeting closed that day, and we traveled on to Fort Wayne, Indiana, to speak in another church. The next morning when the service was over, we went to our hotel room. As soon as I opened the door, I saw the message light was on. With anticipation we called the desk and found that Kim had called and left word for us to call her back immediately.

I dialed the number as we both thanked God out loud that Jesse and Jenny were found and that they were on their way home. When she answered, Kim was elated. She shouted, "Oh, John! Jesse and Jenny are both home! They are sitting on the couch right next to me!"

Not one hair on their heads had been harmed. The man who took them had called Kim and said he didn't know why, but he could not go through with his plans. He had put the children on the first plane back to their mother.

How faithful God is! We are totally convinced that He is the same yesterday, today, and forever. Just as He moved on behalf of Hannah, He moved on our behalf. As quickly as He answered Jephthah, He answered us.

There is not enough space in this book to share every memorial prayer we have made. I have recounted only a few. Memorial prayer has worked for us many times. It is working for us at this very moment, and it will continue working for us until Jesus returns.

Almost daily our ministry receives testimonies from people who have heard me teach about memorial prayer. Those people are comforted as they tell how God has turned into good that which the devil sent for evil. My wife and I are blessed when we receive such mail, for it makes the Scripture come to life. God is truly enabling us to comfort others by sharing with them how He has comforted us.

> . . . we may be able to comfort them . . . by the comfort wherewith we ourselves are comforted of God.
>
> **2 Corinthians 1:4**

I do hope these examples will become a comfort to you. I can, without hesitation, recommend this wonderful way of moving the hand of God to everyone.

11

It Will Work For You

. . . God is no respecter of persons.
Acts 10:34

As you have read this book, I am sure this question must have crossed your mind more than once: "Will memorial prayer work for me?" The answer is, *yes*. There are several reasons that cause me to say so.

You Are Special To God

First, it will work for you because the God we serve is not a respecter of persons. No matter how important or unimportant you may think you are, God has written the Bible to you. If you have been saved, you are His child. He desires to see only good things come into your life.

. . . no good thing will he withhold from them
that walk uprightly.
Psalm 84:11

He wants you to have complete victory.

> **Now thanks be unto God, which always causeth us to triumph in Christ. . . .**
> **2 Corinthians 2:14**

God Has Something Better For You

A second reason I know memorial prayer will work for you is this. Everything God did for those who lived in the Old Testament days, He will do *even better for us today*. The entire Book of Hebrews is dedicated to that theme. There God promised us a better hope, better testament, better covenant, better promises, and even a better sacrifice. Let me say it again. Whatever the saints had in the Old Testament, something even better is available to us under the New Testament.

> **God . . . provided some better thing for us. . . .**
> **Hebrews 11:40**

God Never Changes

A final proof that memorial prayer will work for you is that our great *God never changes*.

> **For I am the Lord, I change not. . . .**
> **Malachi 3:6**

> **Jesus Christ the same yesterday, and to day, and for ever.**
> **Hebrews 13:8**

146

God is the same today as He was in the beginning. What He has done for others, He will do for you.

God Will Move His Hand For You

Is there an area of your life where the hand of God must move? Maybe you have *a wayward child.* The devil likes to get a double benefit from children who choose to operate out of the will of God. He not only ruins the life of the child, but he also breaks the hearts of the parents, and many times the situation destroys their testimony.

Recently I was counseling with a pastor and his wife. They related to me how their best Sunday school worker had a problem. Her daughter had become rebellious and run away from home. The young lady was living as a libertine, drinking and doping openly on the streets of their city. She was nothing more than a public prostitute. Now the pastor and his wife felt they needed to decide about removing the mother from all her responsibilities in the Sunday school.

How happy it made the devil to see the life of the child plunged into the depths of sin, plus the bonus of seeing a great Christian worker disqualified and set on the sidelines. (Let me quickly say, I do not think the Lord would have that good woman removed from service over her daughter's sin, but that is another subject.)

Save The Children

Many parents desperately cry for their wayward children across the length and breadth of Christianity. Everywhere we go, we find those who need to move God's hand in the lives of their children. Maybe you have a great need like that. Memorial prayer can change the situation. It has faithfully brought two of our own children back from the edge of destruction, and now they work full time in the ministry.

If you have wayward children, do not let go of them. Build a memorial prayer before your God that will move His hand and snatch them out of the clutches of the devil. Speak it out boldly to your God. Tell Him of the need for their deliverance. Then give just as boldly, mingling your offering with your prayer. Remember, the Bible says that kind of prayer brings your request perpetually before God.

> . . . thy *prayer is heard,* and thine *alms are had in remembrance in the sight of God.*
> Acts 10:31

> . . . Thy *prayers* and thine *alms* are come up for a *memorial before God.*
> Acts 10:4

A Higher Standard Of Living Is Scriptural

Some of you are sorely pressed upon by *the pressures of insufficiency.* Every month you believe that your

148

quality of life will be made a bit better. Then, month after month you fail to see any significant change. The car you drive gets older. Your clothing needs to be replaced. The chance of your children receiving a proper education becomes slimmer and slimmer with each passing year. You know your job has no hope of advancement. To put it in just a sentence, *you need your needs met in a much better way.*

Don't despair. You can do something about your circumstances. Someone wants your living standard improved. It is your God. He wants your needs properly met.

> . . . his divine power hath given unto us all things that pertain unto *life* and godliness. . . .
> **2 Peter 1:3**

This very day you can form a memorial before God that will bring you into the quality lifestyle you desire — a lifestyle that will provide the good things you need. A well-informed child of God has no scriptural reason to go through life without having a good living standard.

Start today to speak to God of your desire for a better *job,* better *house,* better *car,* and especially a *better future for your children.*

Segmented Giving In Memorial Prayer

The Apostle Paul told us that the Philippians had just such a desire for their lives, and God granted their request when they formed and funded a memorial prayer before Him.

> . . . my God shall supply all your need according to his riches in glory by Christ Jesus.
> **Philippians 4:19**

They accomplished the financial portion of their memorial with segmented giving.

> . . . ye sent once and again unto my necessity.
> **Philippians 4:16**

Many times my wife and I were not financially able to give the amount we wanted to give in one lump sum. In order to keep that lack from hindering us, we sometimes gave smaller amounts (what we could pay) on a regular basis (monthly or weekly). For instance, if we felt we wanted to give $1,000.00 but couldn't afford it, we would give $20.00 a week for fifty weeks.

A little saying I learned many years ago will fit well here. "It's *hard by the yard,* but it's a *cinch by the inch.*" Giving $1,000.00 may be hard, or even impossible to many people, but giving $20.00 a week is not as hard. After fifty weeks, it equals the same amount.

Widows Move The Hand Of God

In the day in which we live, there are millions of broken homes. Single mothers are raising almost half the children in the United States today. They come from all walks of life. Many of them are Christian women. My heart goes out to those special saints, for their need for good Christian men is evident.

As I speak to those dear souls, they tell me they love God and they know He will see them through. Almost all of them tell me that the thing they desire most is *a good, Christian husband* — one who will love their children and be a good father.

If you are a single mother, make a memorial prayer to God for a perfect mate. God can bring forth His man of your dreams. Just begin to speak to Him about your need. Describe the man you and your family desire, then give a memorial offering to God.

God has a special ear for the memorial prayers of single mothers. He immediately moved His hand into the barrel of meal and cruse of oil for the single mother at Zarephath when she mixed her giving with her prayer. He immediately turned His ear to the widow with the two mites when she gave. He will surely hear you when you approach Him with a memorial prayer.

It Works At The Brink Of Disaster

You may be at the very brink of disaster. Friend, let me tell you. God's hand can move to assist you in short order. You may be faced with a deadline, some impossible mountain that must be moved. It may be the eleventh hour of the day, and your high noon encounter with the devourer is but an hour away.

Remember Jephthah. He was faced with the destruction of his entire army. As he looked out upon the battlefield, he saw that the arm of flesh had failed him. In a decisive, last-minute attempt to move the hand of God, he activated his prayer with a vow. It was a desperate moment. There wasn't even time to make an offering. He simply promised what he would give.

You may not have time to give an offering to build your memorial. You may just have to call out your vow to God. I have seen people do that many times, and God has moved again and again.

Be Careful When You Vow

Be advised! I have also seen something dangerous take place. Christians can make vows to God in the day of emergency. Then they forget to pay their vows in the day of victory!

There is an illustration of this that I will never forget. Several years ago, I stood at the hospital bedside of a young man who had been in a horrible automobile accident. The doctors gave no hope for his survival. He was literally breathing his last breaths of life. I heard the boy's father make a memorial prayer that immediately moved God's hand into the room. He cried, "Oh, God! Save my son's life, and I will serve you all the days of my life!"

The boy's vital signs suddenly improved. The doctors took hope, and miraculously, the boy lived. *But his father never kept his vow.*

That man should have known better. Several years before, he was faced with divorce. He came to me and vowed to give our church an amusement park he owned if only God would save his marriage. He went so far as to bring the deed for the property and sign it over. In short order, his wife came home to patch things up. Within a few days of her return, he asked me to give him back the deed. A short time later his wife moved out and finalized the divorce. That marriage was not saved because he did not keep his vow to God.

Today that man is in prison serving a life sentence for murder. Most people cannot understand how a former leading citizen of the community could have committed such a heinous crime. I know what happened. He did not pay his vow to God.

> When thou vowest a vow unto God, defer not to pay it; for he hath no pleasure in *fools:* pay that which thou hast vowed.
>
> Better is it that thou *shouldest not vow*, than that thou shouldest vow and *not pay*.
> Ecclesiastes 5:4,5

I must always caution those who make a vow that they keep it.

God will not let you down if you form a memorial with a vow, just as He did not let Hannah down. God immediately moved His hand to open her womb, and Hannah wisely kept her vow to God by bringing her child, Samuel, to God's house. She received one son, and she gave him away. Then God gave her a houseful of precious children.

Child of God, I know you are convinced that memorials work and that they are scriptural. All you need now is to step out in faith and form your own memorial prayer before God. Please do it today. If you do it in accordance with what the Scripture teaches, you will be delighted at how quickly your answer will come. I am convinced that once you try this method of getting God's attention, you will use it again and again.

Please share your testimony with me. You may write to me at the address in the back of this book. I look forward to hearing of your great success with memorial prayer!

John Avanzini was born in Paramaribo, Surinam, South America, in 1936. He was raised and educated in Texas, and received his doctorate in philosophy from Baptist Christian University, Shreveport, Louisiana. Dr. Avanzini now resides with his wife, Patricia, in Fort Worth, Texas, where he is the Director of His Image Ministries.

Dr. Avanzini's television program, *Principles of Biblical Economics,* is aired five times per day, seven days per week, by more than 550 television stations from coast to coast. He speaks nationally and internationally in conferences and seminars every week. His ministry is worldwide, and many of his vibrant teachings are now available in tape and book form.

Dr. Avanzini is an extraordinary teacher of the Word of God, bringing forth many of the present truths that God is using in these days to prepare the Body of Christ for His triumphant return.

To share your testimony with John Avanzini,
you may write:

John Avanzini
P. O. Box 1057
Hurst, Texas 76053

Other Books
by John Avanzini

Always Abounding
Hundredfold
Powerful Principles of Increase
Rapid Debt-Reduction Strategies
Stolen Property Returned
War On Debt
The Wealth of the World

Available from
your local bookstore,
or from:

HARRISON HOUSE
P. O. Box 35035
Tulsa, OK 74153